GLOBE QUARTOS

THE FLEER

EDWARD SHARPHAM

First printed: London, 1607

This edition prepared by Lucy Munro

GLOBE EDUCATION

NHB

NICK HERN BOOKS
LONDON

www.nickhernbooks.co.uk

GLOBE QUARTOS

This edition of *The Fleer*
first published in Great Britain
as a paperback original in 2006
by Nick Hern Books Limited
14 Larden Road, London W3 7ST

in association with

Globe Education
Shakespeare's Globe, New Globe Walk
London SE1 9DT

Typeset in Aldine-401 by the editor
Printed by CLE Print Ltd, St Ives, Cambs PE27 3LE

A CIP catalogue record for this book is available from
the British Library

ISBN-13 978 1 85459 928 5
ISBN-10 1 85459 928 3

Preface

In 1744/5, Robert Dodsley sought to "snatch some of the best pieces of our old Dramatic Writers from total Neglect and Oblivion". He published sixty-one plays, written before the death of Charles I, in a *Select Collection of Old Plays* in twelve volumes.

In 1995, Globe Education decided to follow Dodsley's example and intitiated a 30-year project to stage readings and record, with professional casts, all the non-Shakespeare plays written for the stage between 1567 and 1642. To date, audiences have been able to hear over 120 plays by Barnes, Haughton, Shirley, Wilkins et al.

Full productions of Beaumont and Fletcher's *The Maid's Tragedy* and Middleton's *A Chaste Maid in Cheapside* were staged in the Globe Theatre's opening season in 1997. Since then, plays by Marlowe and Brome and a second Middleton play have also been produced at the Globe.

The popularity of both readings and productions prompted Globe Education to approach Nick Hern to publish some of the plays that had been revived. The first Globe Quarto was edited by Nick de Somogyi and published in 1998. An Editorial Board, composed of David Scott Kastan, Gordon McMullan and Richard Proudfoot, was established to oversee the series in 1999. My thanks to Thomas L Berger who is now the General Editor of the series.

Globe Education is indebted to all the Globe Quarto editors and to everyone who has helped give new life to old plays in staged readings and in productions. The plays and the editions only have a life, however, if they have an audience and readers. I am therefore grateful to you for buying this edition.

As Dodsley noted to his patron, "but for your Generosity" these plays would have "faln with their Authors into utter Oblivion".

Patrick Spottiswoode
Director, Globe Education

The General Editor's Preface

The plays are presented in texts based on the most reliable originals (usually the first printed editions) fully modernised so as to make them easily usable by modern actors and readers. Editorial correction and emendation is undertaken as required by the state of the original. Extra stage directions, and additions to those of the original that are needed to make the action clear, are enclosed in square brackets. In verse speeches, apostrophes to indicate elision of letters and accents to indicate where a word should be stressed are used where appropriate as a guide to metre. In particular, in verse speeches, the ending '-ed' in participles and past tenses of verbs is retained only where it is to be pronounced as a separate syllable (or after 'i' or 'u', as in 'tried', 'sued'); otherwise it appears as '-'d'. In prose speeches, the ending '-ed' is always spelled out fully, since metrical considerations offer no guide to pronunciation.

Introductory matter includes notes from the director or co-ordinator of the production or reading of the play at the Globe and a brief factual introduction by the editor. Glossarial Notes (more comprehensive than in earlier Globe Quartos and keyed to the text by line numbers) explain difficult or obsolete usages and offer brief comment on other points of interest or obscurity. Departures from the wording of the original are recorded in Textual Notes that identify the source of corrections or editorial emendations. The opening of the text in the original on which the edition is based is reproduced in reduced facsimile. Extra material relevant to the understanding of the play may occasionally be included in an Appendix.

ACKNOWLEDGEMENTS

I am very grateful to Gordon McMullan, who originally asked me to edit *The Fleer*, and to Tom Berger, my general editor, whose scrutiny has saved me from many mistakes. I would also like to thank Tony Bell and the cast of the staged reading, Tanya Pollard for scholarly support and for her exhaustive knowledge of early modern tobacco, Ishtla Singh for advice on linguistics and for commenting on the first draft of the introduction, and Gabriel Egan for his suggestion regarding *pray 'e*. I am particularly grateful to Fiona Ritchie for proof-reading and commenting on the final draft. I would also like to thank the participants in Marta Straznicky's 'Playreading' seminar at the Shakespeare Association of America annual conference in Minneapolis (March 2002), at which some early ideas about *The Fleer* were circulated. Thanks are also due to my students at King's College London and Keele University, who acted as guinea pigs for various drafts of the edition. The illustration was provided by the Beinecke Library, Yale University, and I am very grateful for their efficient help. Finally, I would like to record my debts to C.G. Petter, editor of an old-spelling edition of Sharpham's works, and Alexander Leggatt, author of an extremely valuable introduction to and commentary on Sharpham's plays. All mistakes are, of course, my own.

Lucy Munro
Editor

A Review of the Staged Reading

When I talked to Tony Bell, the co-ordinator, a few days before the staged reading of *The Fleer*, we thought that it would be funny and appealing to an audience, but we worried about the jokes which pepper the script. Would a modern audience laugh at Sharpham's four-hundred-year-old quips, or would they fall horribly flat? These anxieties were underlined at the (single) rehearsal, when one member of the cast, an experienced performer of early modern drama, complained that he couldn't see what might be charming about the play. When the read-through started, however, my apprehensions dissolved, as Sharpham's dialogue lifted from the page in the hands of an excellent cast. (The malcontent actor admitted after about ten minutes that it played much better than it read; I managed not to say, 'I told you so'.)

The play's blocking is relatively straightforward, perhaps as a result of its having been performed originally in an indoor theatre. Potential problems were rather to be found in the negotiation of tone and genre. Although *The Fleer* features murderous schemes and attempts at poisoning, its tone remains light and breezy throughout. The staged reading brought out the play's careful balancing of various kinds of comedy, ranging from monologue and duologue to carefully constructed ensemble sequences. It even introduced an element of slapstick when the Serving-Man in Act Two (doubled by Jonathan McGuinness with the Gentleman Usher) appeared stripped to the waist and wearing handcuffs.

To a large extent, casting was key. The role of Antifront, the deposed Italian duke who disguises himself as a jeering low-life called Fleer, is absolutely crucial to the play, which he dominates to an extent rare in children's company plays. Between the end of the first act and the end of the fifth, Antifront/Fleer hardly leaves the stage; scarcely two hundred lines are spoken out of his presence and he has more than three times the number of lines of any other character. His speech is also hugely varied. After one scene in iambic pentameter, in which the newly usurped duke discusses his situation with a loyal nobleman, Antifront reappears in the persona of Fleer, swapping his verse for lively prose. Later in the play he adopts further disguises as an Italian apothecary and a judge.

The Globe's Antifront, Geoffrey Freshwater, had the advantage of coming to us fresh from performing in the Royal Shakespeare Company's first 'Jacobethan' season, in which he played Touchstone in Chapman, Jonson and Marston's *Eastward Ho* and Bilioso in Marston's *The Malcontent*. Both of these plays were performed by the Children of the Revels, the company that first acted *The Fleer*; *The Malcontent* is an important source for Sharpham's play, helping to shape its narrative structure and satiric tone. In particular, the reading caught perfectly Sharpham's desire to remind us of the emotional ties which undercut the excesses of the on-stage satirist and underline Antifront/Fleer's manipulation of his daughter-employers.

In the most rewarding of the younger male roles, Russell Layton as Petoune and David Tennant as Piso were superbly funny. Each of these characters has set-piece scenes which give the actor real scope: Petoune's rejection at the hands of Nan and Susan and his later courtship of the elderly Fromaga; Piso's violent expressions of love for Florida and his parodic prison monologue in Act Five, Scene Three. Care was taken to cast attractive comic performers in the less showy roles: Barnaby Kay and Alan Cox as the gallants Spark and Ruffle, and James Tucker as Sir John Have-Little. This casting was crucial to the success of comic sequences such as the interrogation of Fleer at the end of Act One, and Spark and Ruffle's discussion of their visions of hell in Act Five, Scene Four.

Like many plays written for children's companies, *The Fleer* includes a number of rewarding female roles. These are carefully delineated and contrasted, the decadent noblewomen Florida and Felecia, with their sophistic acceptance of their immoral trade, being juxtaposed with the witty, chaste and down-to-earth gentlewomen, Nan and Susan. Performance also highlighted for me the subtly shaded difference between Florida (Mairead Carty) and Felecia (Claire Price): the former was more confident and assertive – seen in the way in which she takes the lead in their discussion of prostitution – the latter a little more uncertain. As Nan and Susan, Hermione Gulliford and Michelle Butterly brought out the lively comedy of their humiliation of Petoune and the comic pathos of their inability to serve the right gentlemen in their disguises as boys. And Carol MacReady as Fromaga, Florida and Felecia's waiting gentlewoman, handled her innuendo-laden dialogue with a real lightness of touch, preventing the character from being a mere grotesque and making her courtship with Petoune almost touching.

Unusually for a Read Not Dead staged reading, *The Fleer* actually received a review; 'What a treat!' said *Whatsonstage.com*, describing it as a 'zesty run-through' which was worth the cost of a ticket for 'the quality cast alone'.

Lucy Munro

THE FLEER

Cast of the staged reading at the Globe Education Centre, 20 June 2004, co-ordinated by Tony Bell

Lord	Jonathan McGuinness
Antifront	Geoffrey Freshwater
Florida	Mairead Carty
Felecia	Claire Price
Fromaga	Carol MacReady
Gentleman	Jonathan McGuinness
Susan	Michelle Butterly
Nan	Hermione Gulliford
Spark	Barnaby Kay
Ruffle	Alan Cox
Sir John Have-Little	James Tucker
Lord Piso	David Tennant
Petoune	Russell Layton
Alunio	Jeremy Harrison
Mittimus	Jonathan McGuinness
First Jailor	Jeremy Harrison
Judge Caius	Jonathan McGuinness
Second Judge	Michael George Moore
Messenger	Jeremy Harrison
Musicians	Jeremy Harrison
	Michael George Moore

Jailors, Serving-men and Messengers played by members of the company

EDITOR'S INTRODUCTION

On its first publication in 1607, Edward Sharpham's *The Fleer* was advertised as 'it hath beene often played in the *Blacke-Fryers* by the Children of the Revells'. The Children of the Revels, formerly known as the Children of the Queen's Revels, were the most influential and contentious of the early Jacobean children's companies, frequently in trouble with the authorities for satirising King and court. In 1606, the year of the first performances of *The Fleer*, they lost the patronage of James' queen consort, Anna of Denmark, in the furore over John Day's incendiary play *The Isle of Gulls*, in the aftermath of which several of the company were imprisoned.

Originally from Devon and a member of the Middle Temple, Sharpham was one of the many members of the Inns of Court who tried his hand at writing for the theatre. *The Fleer* is his first extant play. His second, *Cupid's Whirligig*, was performed by the short-lived Children of the King's Revels at the Whitefriars Theatre around 1607-8, but his career was cut short in a savage outbreak of plague in spring 1608. Sharpham succumbed to the disease on 22 April; the epidemic also put the Children of the King's Revels out of business and – together with further political indiscretions – all but destroyed the Children of the Revels.

The preface to the first edition of *The Fleer* is at pains to emphasise the play's popularity and comedic worth. *The Fleer* is 'like forfeits to a usurer, long looked-for'; it is 'a book … to make you laugh, and lie down too, if you please', and 'in this modicum you may conceive [Sharpham's] great desire to delight you' ('To the Reader and Hearer', ll. 7-8, 3-4, 22-3). Early readers of the play evidently agreed: *The Fleer* went through three further editions before 1635, and a number of its best jokes were recycled in a 1639 jest-book, *Conceits, Clinches, Flashes and Whimzies*.

It also seems to have been popular on the stage. A copy of the first edition, now owned by the British Library (BL 11773.c.8), has been abridged for performance in a seventeenth-century hand, and there is also a tantalising reference to the play's final act in Anthony Nixon's *A Strange Foot-Post* (London, 1613): 'The Cooke will put poison in his porridge, or worke him some other mischiefe, if he durst: then enters the Fleire like the *Chorus* in a Tragedy, and telleth all' (sig. F4v). Unless Nixon is drawing on old memories, this may indicate that *The Fleer* was revived around 1612, possibly by the reconstituted Children of the Queen's Revels, who had taken over the Whitefriars theatre and performed a number of Blackfriars plays in revival.

The Fleer is one of a group of early Jacobean plays that have become known as 'disguised-ruler plays'. It is indebted to John Marston's *The Malcontent*, performed by the Children of the Queen's Revels and the King's Men in 1602-4, and to the King's Men's own *Measure for Measure* (1603-4). In particular, *The Fleer* seems to have been designed to fill a gap left in the Queen's Revels repertory by the disappearance of Marston's *The Fawn* (1604-5), which had been taken to a rival company, the Children of Paul's. Where Marston's play features a duke who disguises himself as a character called Fawn – the embodiment of courtly flattery – Sharpham's features a duke who disguises himself as a character called Fleer, the embodiment of fleering or jeering plain speech. In *The Fawn*, Hercules leaves his dukedom to spy on his son Tiberio, trying to regulate the latter's lack of passion and steer him into an advantageous marriage. In *The Fleer*, Antifront has been deposed from his dukedom and spies on his daughters, Florida and Felecia, who are working as prostitutes; he acts as their pander but eventually regulates their excess of passion and steers them into advantageous marriages. Unlike *The Fawn*, however, *The Fleer* catapults an Italian duke into contemporary London, using his scabrous disguise-persona to analyse and comment on contemporary politics and social affairs.

In view of the importance of the disguised-ruler motif to the play, it is intriguing to find that the reviser of the British Library text was completely unconcerned with it, perhaps suggesting a short theatrical fashion for such story-lines. In the new version, Antifront is not a disguised ruler, but a cynical servant; it is not surprising that the adapter seems to have had problems with the play's conclusion, in which the disguised ruler reveals himself, and it is unlikely that the adaptation was ever performed as it stands.

Like Marston and Shakespeare, Sharpham uses the disguised-ruler motif to discuss the relationship between court and city and, in the tradition of the Children of the Revels, he makes a number of specific jibes against courtiers in general and King James's notorious 'thirty-pound knights' in particular. The assertion that the play will be 'sweet in the palates of your minds – though your mouths may find it bitter in digestion' ('To the Reader and Hearer', ll. 24-5) suggests a satiric edge that has been blunted a little in transmission. Cuts appear to have been imposed, notably at 2.1.311, where Ruffle asks Antifront/Fleer to explain why the cuckolding of the courtiers by the citizens will make the court grow rich, but does not wait for a reply.

In a judgement typical of critical attitudes towards Sharpham's work, Felix Schelling described *The Fleer* as 'foully if wittily effective' (*Elizabethan Drama 1558-1642*, 2 vols [Boston: Houghton, Mifflin & Co., 1908], 1: 518). As Schelling suggests, a great deal of the play's pleasure comes from its jokes, and in particular from its cheerful obscenity. Despite the exhilaratingly foul-tempered presence of Antifront/Fleer in almost every scene, however, the play is in some respects remarkably genial. The presentation of the love-lorn sisters Susan and Nan is sympathetic but their wit prevents them from becoming cloying. The foolish, tobacco-addicted gallant Petoune is perhaps the epitome of Sharpham's double-edged treatment of his material. He is satirised as a syphilitic, a scapegoat for the sexual behaviour of the majority of the cast, but is nonetheless appealing in his generally tolerant reaction to the mockery he suffers throughout the play. As thought-provoking entertainment, *The Fleer* deserves greater attention than it has generally been granted.

Lucy Munro

The Fleer

To the Reader and Hearer

Friendly perusers or perusing friends, that have been over-bold with some of us, give me leave to be a little bold with you. I have printed a book here to make you laugh, and lie down too, if you please. I know it comes not like a mouse-trap, to inveigle your good opinions, nor like news of great armies, very strange and undreamt of, but like forfeits to a usurer, long looked-for. If you find any errors by me committed, correct them or neglect them. The author is invisible to me; viz. i'th' country, but whereabouts I cannot learn. Yet I fear he will see me too soon, for I had of him before his departure an epistle or apological preamble (this being his first Minerva) directed unto you, which should have been in this page divulged. And – not to jest with you because this book plays that part sufficiently – I have lost it, remembering none of the contents. And therefore, kind readers, I do presume thus to salute you. Use these comical discourses favourably and you shall have some from the author hereafter more worthy your favours and affections; through a narrow window you may view a broad field, so in this modicum you may conceive his great desire to delight you. But, howsoever, I know this volume will be sweet in the palates of your minds – though your mouths may find it bitter in digestion – and so I commit your eyes to the next page.

Dramatis Personae
in order of appearance

Florentine LORD ANTIFRONT	*Former Duke of Florence; later disguised as Fleer*
FLORIDA	*Elder daughter of Antifront*
FELECIA	*Younger daughter of Antifront*
FROMAGA	*Waiting gentlewoman to Florida and Felecia*
GENTLEMAN	*Protégé of Sir John Have-Little; later gentleman usher to Florida and Felecia*
SUSAN, NAN	*Sisters*
SPARK, RUFFLE	*Gallants*
Sir John HAVE-LITTLE	*An impecunious knight*
Lord PISO	*Heir to the new Duke of Florence*
PETOUNE	*A foolish gallant*
SERVING-MAN	*Serves Florida and Felecia*
ALUNIO	*A Florentine apothecary*
MITTIMUS	*Justice Ferrio's clerk*
FIRST JAILOR	
Judge CAIUS	
SECOND JUDGE	
SECOND JAILOR	
MESSENGER	

Serving-men

[Act 1, Scene 1]

Enter Signor ANTIFRONT, *with a* LORD

Lord
Dear Lord, I know it well becomes not me
To counsel him that best can counsel me;
Yet if it please you but to lend your ears
And hear my love, if not my counsel –

Antifront
No more.
I know thy love tends to the stopping
Of my longing and my resolution.
Thou know'st that I no longer now am Signor;
Florence hath got another governor,
And one step back in state of majesty is a greater fall
Than to a meaner man that looseth all.
Besides, thou know'st our daughters they are fled,
The true inheritors of Florence right,
And mighty Piso now usurps our regal seat;
Puissant in power and mighty in his wrong
Hath mounted falcon-like into the sky of state,
Seized on our feebleness and beat our weakness down.
And therefore now I am resolv'd
To find my two lost children out,
Or like as Phaeton in pride did ride,
So I in grief will pace the world about.

Lord
Unto your celsitude I wish,
Till their effects your hopes may never fail. *Exit*

Antifront
Farewell. Some strange disguise I needs must take
Both for my stealth away as for my passage on the way.

And yet my fortunes fall; disguisement is too great
If pleased the heavens, but their wills still are laws:
All is but justice and our sins the cause.
Cuor forte rompe cativa sorte. *Exit*

[1.2]

Enter FLORIDA *and* FELECIA, *daughters to Signor* ANTIFRONT, *Madam* FROMAGA *their waiting gentlewoman, and two or three* SERVING-MEN

Florida Withdraw! Leave us – we would be private.

Exeunt all but [FLORIDA *and* FELECIA]

Sister, what think you of this trade of ours?

Felecia 'Tis base to be a whore.

Florida 'Tis base to abuse great place or baseness to deceive great trust.

Felecia And is't not baseness to abuse great birth?

Florida Yes, if great birth abused not us. If Piso had not proved the thief, and robbed us of our right, 't had been worse than theft in us to rob ourselves of honour. You'll say we are forbid to live by sin, and yet we are commanded to seek to live; the letter law express forbids to kill, and yet the sense permits it rather than be killed. And since of two extremities the least is to be chosen, you know we have no other means to live. But had we, yet we are fair by nature, scorning art, and was not beauty made to be enjoyed? Do we not exclaim on those who have abundant store of coin and yet for want suffer the needy perish at their door? So might all do on us, having so much beauty, if we should suffer men for love of us to die; shall we in whom beauty keeps her court be curbed and tied to one man's benevolence? No, no, not I. Rather than in virtue to live poor, in sin I'll die.

Felecia Your resolutions hath confirmed my doubts and, since 'tis hateful to live poor, to maintain our state I am content. But these observances let us keep: strangely 'mongst strangers let us hold our state and let our servants seldom know how familiar with our friends we be, and though England's wealth do now adorn us, let's keep the fashion still of Florence.

Florida Content, let's in. Who's near? Attend us, ho!

[*Exeunt*]

[1.3]

Enter FROMAGA [*as* FLORIDA *and* FELECIA] *exeunt; to her enter a* GENTLEMAN

Gentleman This is the street, and, as I remember, this is the door. I'll ask this ancient gentlewoman. [*to* FROMAGA] Health and beauty dwell with you, lady.

Fromaga I thank you sir. [*aside*] 'A has a courtly phrase, i'faith.

Gentleman Do the Florentine ladies dwell here?

Fromaga Yes, forsooth, sir, I am a poor gentlewoman that follows 'em.

Gentleman I am sent to 'em by a knight, who promised me

he had procured me the place of a gentleman usher to them.

Fromaga Sir John Have-Little, I think.

Gentleman Yes, indeed, the same.

Fromaga [*aside*] By my troth, he's an honest knight; 'a has no fault but that he's poor and that's a small fault nowadays. [*to* GENTLEMAN] But let me see, sir, I pray, were you never a gentleman usher before?

Gentleman No, truly, never yet.

Fromaga Then you must be instructed, sir.

Gentleman I shall be glad to learn.

Fromaga I hope you and I shall be more inward, sir, and for your instruction I shall be glad to lay open any secrets that I have. Therefore first you must observe – ha' you any tables?

Gentleman Yes, sure, I never go without tables.

Fromaga Pluck out your pin and write down as I shall utter. To be always ready – standing bare – to be employed when, where, and howsoever your ladies please. You must never be without money of your own to lay out when your ladies bid you, as eighteen pence to the porter, half a crown to the coachman, or twelve pence for a torch if their ladyships come home late at night. If you be sent by your lady to another lady to know what rest she took i'th' night, you shall deliver your answer just as it came from the lady. You must always be in a clean band and clean cuffs, how foul soe'er your shirt be.

Gentleman I will observe all this.

Fromaga You may by virtue of your office wear a periwig, provided it be just of the colour of your beard. Let me see, you have a hatched sword of your own there, have ye not?

Gentleman Yes, forsooth, I bought it for his ladyships' service.

Fromaga 'Twas well done, you may wear it by your office. What, is your cloak lined through?

Gentleman No, but 'tis of a good depth in.

Fromaga 'Tis well done too: your ladies love to have it lined a good depth in, 'tis for their credit. What, are these silver hangers of your own?

Gentleman No, I borrowed these. But I have a pair of mine own.

Fromaga They are in trouble, are they?

Gentleman No, truly, they are at mending.

Fromaga Nay, though they be 'tis no shame. You have been long out of service, perchance.

Gentleman Some three months.

Fromaga By'r Lady, 'tis a long time. But can you endure to walk some half a day in the hall or the great chamber, while some great lord is busy with your lady in an inner room? You may sleep an hour or two, as your citizens' wives do at a sermon, to pass away the time, but you must have a care to wake at the rushing of a satin gown or the creaking of a door, that if your lady come you may be presently up and bare.

Gentleman Yes, sure, I could do it well.

Enter FLORIDA

Fromaga You must stand stiff up and hold up your head: 'tis the chiefest thing belongs to your place. Look, here comes the elder lady. [*to* FLORIDA] Madam, here's the gentleman that Sir John Have-Little commended to your ladyship for a gentleman usher.

Florida Let him draw near us.

Gentleman [*to* FLORIDA] The knight commends his dear affection, and by me makes tender of his humble service to your ladyship.

Fromaga [*to* GENTLEMAN] Kiss your hand and go forward upon her.

[GENTLEMAN] *delivers a letter*
[*and* FLORIDA *reads it*]

Florida We accept it, have read it. You are beholding to the knight, and he hath spared no pains to make your worthy parts well known to us. Draw near us; henceforth we accept you as our own, and so we bid you welcome. Are you a gentleman?

Gentleman Yes, sure, Madam, for I was both born and begotten in an inn's court.

Fromaga Sure, Madam, then he's a gentleman; for he that's but admitted to the house is a gentleman, much more he that's begotten in the house.

Florida You are the more welcome, and our bounty shall deserve your industry. *Exit* FLORIDA

Gentleman Is the lady a princess, that she speaks 'us' and 'we' so much?

Fromaga No, she says so meaning herself and her sister, for they are both one, and such things as they have they use in common, and must stand bare before them both. Look, here comes the t'other lady.

Enter FELECIA

[*to* FELECIA] Madam, here's the gentleman that Sir John Have-Little commended to your ladyship for a gentleman usher.

Felecia We like him and he's welcome. [*to* GENTLEMAN] What good parts have you? Have you the tongues?

Gentleman Not very well, Madam.

Fromaga Yes, Madam, 'a has the Scottish tongue very perfectly, and 'a has some skill in the Irish tongue too.

Felecia That's a wild speech.

Fromaga Nay, I'll warrant your ladyship he'll not run away. Has travelled, Madam, too, 'a says, for 'a has been in Wales.

Felecia Has 'a no skill in the French tongue?

Gentleman Some little skill, Madam.

Fromaga No, sure, Madam, I think your ladyship hath more knowledge of the French than he.

Felecia Well, we will at more leisure survey your good parts, and make thereof the best for our own use. *Exit*

Gentleman I pray 'e what wages do these ladies give?

Fromaga Faith, your wages will be much about the nature of your office, very bare standing wages; I think some forty shillings a year.

Gentleman Why, how mean they I shall live in their service?

Fromaga Why, by their countenance. I ha' known a lord hath given his fool nothing but his countenance to live by, and I can tell you 't 'as proved a good court-maintenance too.

Gentleman Countenance? I hope I have a countenance good enough of mine own, I need not serve for one.

Fromaga [*aside*] In troth and so 'a has for a gentleman usher, I must needs say a very harmless silly countenance.

Gentleman Yet, faith, I mean to try their bounty.

Fromaga Come, will you walk in, sir? I'll follow you.

Gentleman Very willingly.

Fromaga [*aside*] This is brave, i'faith, 'a shall go bare before me too; 'a will serve us all three when we are abroad. *Exeunt*

[1.4]

Enter Mistress SUSAN, *and* NAN, *sisters*

Susan Come, sister, come – we were not born to stand, 'tis against the nature of our sex's kind. Come, sit, and tell me how many suitors you have, and which you most do love, and I will tell you all mine, and which I most respect.

Nan Faith, I have a dozen at the least, and their deserts are all so good, I know not which I

should love most. And one last day did court me thus:
'Oh, had my tongue the influence to lead
Thy fair thoughts as thy fair looks do mine:
Then should'st thou be his prisoner who is thine.'
I, seeing my poor gentleman likely to be drowned in the depth of Hellespont, delivered him this verse to catch hold of:
'Oh, be not fair, and so unkind: misshapen stuff
Is of behaviour boisterous and rough.'

Susan But come, what was 'a for a man?

Nan What was 'a for a man? Why, 'a was a man for a woman, what should 'a be? And i'faith he was a neat lad too, for his beard was newly cut bare; marry, it showed something like a meadow newly mowed: stubble, stubble.

Susan Well, I have a suitor too. If he had as much wit as living, it may be I should find in my heart to love him.

Nan What, is't Sir John Have-Little, that gallant knight that courts delicate ladies? 'Spare not the sweat of my body. Man was made to labour (use my creation), women to bear (I'll use yours); birds to fly, fish to swim', et cetera, and then swears, 'By my conscience lady, I esteem you as I do money, which buys everything'. And that's but like a punk, for every man has to do with it.

Susan No, sister, no! 'Tis not he, for I think his wit cannot call his wealth master, nor his wealth his wit, and yet they are both servants to a fool.

Nan Faith, who is't, sister? Is't a proper man? Hath he a good face?

Susan 'Tis the person and conditions I respect, and not face; for every boy has a good face and it's not worth a hair. No, sister, no. My love is more worthier than words can utter; I cannot sympathize his rare perfections with any earthly substance. This globe of dirt produceth nothing worthy of his comparison; his soul's perfection so refines his body, as you would think an angel were his sire. His discourse, behaviour and humanity attracts to him my soul's felicity.

Nan [*aside*] Pray heaven it be not mine.
[*to* SUSAN] Nay, come, who is your love? Tell me!

Susan Nay, who is yours? Speak first!

Nan Yet again!

Susan [*aside*] If it be mine, my heart will break.
[*to* NAN] Mine is Master –

Nan Who, who, who?

Susan Ruffle.

Nan Pray God't be true.

Susan In troth, 'tis he.

Nan And mine is Master Spark, and look here they come.

Enter SPARK, RUFFLE, PISO, [HAVE-LITTLE] *and* PETOUNE

Spark Faith, ladies, youth and beauty always be your handmaids.

Ruffle Best fortunes your attendants.

Piso Good clothes your companions.

Ruffle We all of us your servants.

Petoune And let tobacco be your perfumes.

Nan Lord, gentlemen, how your wits caper! Methinks ’twould become you well at first entrance, your discretions came in with a sober measure.

Spark Ladies, we are come to make a gentleman of your acquaintance here.

Nan His name, good Master Spark? He’s very welcome.

Spark His name is Signor Petoune, a traveller and a great tobacconist.

Petoune Faith, ladies, I take it now and then fasting for the purification of my wit.

Susan Purification? Why, has your wit lain in child-bed, sir?

Ruffle Yes indeed, lady, brought to bed of a moon-calf.

Petoune Faith, ladies, if you used but a-mornings when ye rise the divine smoke of this celestial herb, it will more purify, cleanse and mundify your complexions by ten parts than your dissolved mercury, your juice of lemons, your distilled snails, your gourd waters, your oil of tartar or a thousand such toys.

Spark Sure ladies, I must needs say th’instinct of this herb hath wrought in this gentleman such a divine influence of good words, excellent discourse, admirable invention, incomparable wit. Why, I tell ye, when he talks, wisdom stands a mile off and dares not come near him for fear 'a should shame her. But before 'a did use this tobacco, 'a was the arrantest woodcock that ever I saw.

Petoune Indeed, I was a very silly fellow.

Ruffle Nay, you were an arrant ass.

Petoune Sure, I was a fool.

Have-Little Nay, you were a most monstrous puppy.

Petoune Indeed, I was an idiot, a very idiot.

Piso By this light, thou wert a most egregious coxcomb.

Petoune Indeed I was, indeed I was.

Spark But since, it hath embellished his good parts, perfected his ill parts, and made his secret actions correspondent to his outward wisdom, as you may well perceive.

Petoune Faith, lady, these gentlemen have not long used my company, yet you see how tobacco hath already refined their spirits.

Piso Petoune, I wonder tobacco hath not purified the complexion of thy nose.

Petoune Why, what ails my nose?

Piso Nay, be not angry, I do not touch thy nose to th'end 'a should take anything in snuff.

Petoune Why do y' play so about my nose?

Have-Little 'Tis a good turn he's no fly, Signor; if 'a were, 'a would burn his wings.

Nan O Signor, these gentlemen have not long used your company, yet you see how tobacco hath already refined their spirits.

Petoune [*to* NAN] Faith, lady, would you bestow but one favour of me?

Nan Truly, Signor, if you should have as much favour as you have complexion, you would be highly favoured.

Petoune Dear lady, now by this day I love you.

Nan Cheap Signor, now by the light of this day I cannot love you.

Spark Now, lady, what drugs of wit has this apothecary of tobacco sold you?

Nan Faith, 'a sold me none, sir, only 'a gave me a taste of his good meaning.

Petoune [*to* SUSAN] Faith, lady, I must enquire your name.

Susan I pray 'e do, sir: yond' gentlewoman knows it.

Petoune Oh, I know it well enough.

Susan Why do you enquire it then?

Petoune Come come, lady, can you love?

Susan Aye.

Petoune And can you love me?

Susan No.

Petoune Every fool can say aye and no.

Susan And I always answer every fool so.

Petoune Do y'think I want wit?

Susan If you do, 'tis a shame you do not learn it.

Petoune Will you teach me? I'll come to you to school.

Susan 'Tis not my profession, sir, to teach a fool.

Spark Look, look – this fellow is like your upright shoe; he will serve either foot.

Petoune Good lady, have a better regard of me. Do but think me made of the same mettle other men are.

Susan If others were of the same metal you are, and all mine, I should quickly sell them to the bell-makers.

Petoune Why, what mettle do you think me?

Susan Copper, sir, copper, for I take your body to be of the same metal your nose is.

Petoune Dear lady, now by this day I love you.

Spark Why, how now Signor? What says the lady? Will she love thee, man?

Petoune Faith, I can get but a cold comfort of her.

Spark Well, thank her for't.

Petoune For what?

Spark Why, for her cold comfort – she gave it thee to cool the heat of thy nose, man.

Susan Signor, you see these gentlemen have not long used your company, yet you see how tobacco hath already refined their spirits.

Ruffle Why, how now Signor? At blind man's buff? Bobbed on either side?

Petoune Prithee peace. [*to* SUSAN] Dear lady, please you take a pipe of tobacco?

Ruffle Aye, come; I'll begin to her. [RUFFLE *puffs on the pipe*] Why, what a rogue art thou to offer a fair lady an empty pipe!

Susan Why, Signor, do you make a fool of me?

Piso Had you nobody, Signor, to have bobbed with an empty pipe but her?

Nan Why, how now, Signor? Could you find never a fitter block to whet your wit on but my sister?

Spark By the divine smoke of tobacco, Signor, you have shamed us all.

Petoune Swear not, good sir, swear not! Profane not the Indian plant!

Have-Little Had you nobody else, Signor, to break an empty jest on but this lady?

Susan No, no, 'a thinks anything is good enough for me.

Petoune [*to* SPARK] Sir, would you make my lady and me friends?

Spark Nay, Signor, I have no face to speak now you have abused her in your own element. If it had been in anything but tobacco, I would have done my best.

Ruffle Hark you, Signor, you were best to ask her forgiveness on your knees. There's no way to get her friendship else.

Petoune But will she forgive me, think you, if I ask her mercy on my knees?

Spark Why, prove, Signor; you can but try. We'll all speak for you. [PETOUNE *kneels*]

Ruffle [*to* SUSAN] Good lady, will you forgive this Signor? You see his penitent grief hath brought him very low, for he's on's knees; besides, he weeps. [*to* PETOUNE] Speak, Signor, speak for yourself!

Petoune Lady, I must confess, I have offered you an empty pipe, which methinks hath small reason to be taken in snuff.

Spark And you are sorry for't, Signor, are you not?

Petoune Aye, with all my heart.

Spark [*to* SUSAN] Forgive him, good lady, pray forgive him.

Susan I am content, gentlemen, at your entreaties – upon conditions.

Petoune Upon any conditions.

Susan But you shall be sworn to them.

Petoune Most willingly.

Ruffle Come, 'a shall be sworn on's own tobacco pipe.

Piso Look you, Signor, he told you there was no way to get her good will but by kneeling, for he that will have a woman's love must stoop.

Susan Come, Master Ruffle, you shall take his oath and I'll minister't.

Ruffle Come, Signor, put your hand to the pipe.

Susan [*to* PETOUNE] First, you shall never while you live offer lady or gentlewoman an empty pipe.

Petoune Never.

Susan Secondly, you shall never make tobacco your idol, taking it in a morning before you say your prayers.

Petoune Never.

Susan Thirdly, you shall never in the praise of tobacco disclose or dispraise, by the way of making comparisons, the secrets of ladies or gentlewomen, as repeating their distilled waters, their censing oils, or their smoothing unguents.

Spark To this you swear.

Petoune Most willingly.

Susan Fourthly, you shall never come with your squibs and smoke-squirts amongst ladies and gentlewomen, flinging out fume at your nostrils as a whale doth salt-water, unless you be entreated by them.

Petoune Never.

Susan Fifthly, you shall presently convey yourself out of our company, never to come more near us unless you be sent for.

Petoune Never?

Susan No, never. [*to* RUFFLE] So, let him kiss the pipe.

Spark [*to* PETOUNE] Come, Signor, you have kneeled to a fair end, to get you a mistress, and here you have forsworn her.

Petoune I'm in a fair case now.

Piso I'faith, now th'art a comb for any case.

Petoune Well, I'll keep my oath. Farewell gentlemen.

Piso Farewell Signor.

Spark Adieu Signor.

Have-Little God be w'ye Signor.

Petoune Well, some shall smoke for this.

Ruffle Let it be your nose then, good Signor, in any case. *Exit* [PETOUNE]

Enter Signor ANTIFRONT *disguised, called Fleer*

Antifront It's a good soil, a wholesome air, a pretty town, handsome slight buildings, well-proportioned people, very fair women.

Spark Hey-day, this is like a lawyer's study in the latter end of a term: one's no sooner thrunged out, but another's thrust in. Y'are welcome, sir.

Antifront But I am not, sir, for I am sick.

Ruffle Would you speak with any man here?

Antifront I care not greatly, sir, if I spoke with every man here.

Nan He's a mad fellow!

Spark What art?

Antifront Poor.

Ruffle Dost mean to live in this town?

Antifront I'd be loath to die in't.

Have-Little In what country wert born?

Antifront In none.

Have-Little Where then?

Antifront In a town.

Have-Little What nation art?

Antifront An Italian.

Have-Little Oh, then thou canst make glasses.

Antifront Aye, and as wise men as you asses, too! [*aside*] Oh, are you there, Piso? Your father is my good lord, but no more of that yet.

Spark Why Signor, I hope you wonnot swagger!

Antifront No, nor I care not greatly for them that do; for your swaggerer is but like your walking spur, 'a jingles much but he'll never prick.

Have-Little Why art so melancholy?

Susan I'll hold my life he is in love with some waiting gentlewoman.

Antifront He's a mad fellow will love any of you all longer than a pissing while.

Piso Why cam'st thou out of Italy into England?

Antifront Because England would not come into Italy to me.

Piso Why art sad?

Antifront Because I have cause.

Piso Who dost follow?

Antifront My nose.

Spark Who dost serve?

Antifront God.

Ruffle Who art towards?

Antifront He that's before me.

Spark What dost want?

Antifront Money.

Spark Nothing else?

Antifront Yes.

Spark What?

Antifront A good service.

Spark Shall I prefer thee?

Antifront I cannot tell, 'tis as I like the man.

Spark Nay't shall be to a couple of gentlewomen of thine own country.

Antifront I shall have enough to do then, I hope; I have heard of one woman hath served ten men, but I never heard that one man should be preferred to serve two women before! Y'are an Englishman?

Spark Aye.

Antifront So I thought indeed. You cannot poison so well as we Italians, but you'll find a means to bring a man out of his life as soon. God's light! Serve two women, quoth you?

Spark Why, thou shalt serve but one, yet take thy choice of both.

Antifront Aye, marry, sir, I like when't comes to choosing.

Spark What's thy name?

Antifront Fleer.

Spark What's thy profession?

Antifront I have ever been a courtier.

Spark A courtier! Come, gentlemen, I like this fellow so well that I'll prefer him straight.

Nan Do so, you shall do a deed of charity in't.

Spark Fair ladies, you'll excuse us.

Susan You have been very welcome, gentlemen.

Exeunt [SPARK, RUFFLE, HAVE-LITTLE, PISO and ANTIFRONT,] SUSAN [*and*] NAN [*remain*]

Nan Come, sister, there rests nothing for us now but this: we'll get us men's apparel, and serve them as pages. So shall we hinder them in their marriages, and in th'end prefer ourselves to be their wives.

Susan I like it well. Come, let's about it presently.

Exeunt

[Act 2, Scene 1]

Enter [ANTIFRONT *alone,*] *in a new suit*

Antifront I have not yet been seven days here and yet I see that grieves my very soul. My daughters – my ladies I must say now – make lust labour for their maintenance, and this foolish nation will sell their goods, their lands – nay, their very souls – for night's delights and momentary sports, which like to lightning appears and vanisheth ere one can say 'tis come. But then repentance sticks close. There was a fellow with one of my ladies this morning, and the poor slave has but seven shillings a week board wages, and yet he has given six on't for a bit of extraordinary flesh. Well, God give him the grace to pray, for 'a must fast. I asked the hot slave why 'a did not marry since 'a could not bridle his lust? And 'a told me 'a had rather fall into the surgeon's mercy than the world's beggary. Well, I see it cannot be denied: mercenary women are necessary members. They pluck down the pride of the flesh yet are not proud themselves, for they'll be as familiar with the men as with the master. They do as many good deeds as some friar that puts one to penance for his sins: they put twenty to pains. He out of charity sends one to the hospital once a year, they send twenty to the surgeons once a month; say he bids men repent, they make 'em repent. Yet for all this some will call 'em damned punks. Well, if they be damned, they'll not be damned *gratis* like your young country gentlemen, nor in hugger-mugger like your citizen's wife with her prentice. They can practise without an overseer: they scorn to have a suburban bawd lend 'em a taffaty gown, and they – like your common players – let men come in for two pence apiece and yet themselves to have but the tenth penny, like the tenth pig. Yet, faith, the trade is a good trade. They forswear not themselves in commendation of their wares, as your common tradesmen do, swearing they cannot afford it at the price. They are no proverb breakers: beware the buyer, say they, you shall have enough for your money; if half will not serve your turn, take the whole; measure by your own yard, you shall have Winchester measure. I was somewhat bold with one of their ladyships this morning and asked her why women went to the generating sport all the year, since beasts themselves went to't but once? And she answered me, because they were women and had reason to know what was good for themselves and so had not beasts. But soft, here comes Signor Petoune –

Enter PETOUNE *taking tobacco*

Petoune O Fleer, how dost, Fleer?

Antifront Oh, Signor, you may snuff out your smoke here, Signor, and save your oath too; here are no cuckold-makers!

Petoune What are they, Fleer?

Antifront Women, Signor, women. I heard what a rash gentleman you are to forswear your mistress's company in the very heat of your affection.

Petoune Hang her, hang her, she's a very cricket. She hath written for me three or four times, but I'll see her damned ere I'll come to her. Woot take any tobacco, Fleer?

Antifront No, not I. I'll not make my nose a red herring: I'll not hang him i'th' smoke.

Petoune Thou art a good courtier, Fleer, th'ast got a suit already.

Antifront Nay, I have two or three offices too.

Petoune Prithee, what are they?

Antifront Why I am Yeoman o'th' Jurden, Gentleman o'th' Smock and Squire of Entertainment. For when your gallants approach, I take their income; for if I stay till their outcome, the devil a bit of any silver, sir, can I get: for your new-made gallants lay all on the back and spend all o'th' belly.

Petoune How do thy two ladies live, Fleer?

Antifront Like two musk-cats in a coop.

Petoune Why, I hear say they live gallantly.

Antifront Phew! They? Why, they keep a little court.

Petoune And what art thou? A sumner?

Antifront A sumner, why?

Petoune Because thou art one of them – hark in thine ear – [*whispers*]

Antifront Well said, calf! Hast been a-sucking all this

while for that jest? No, I have an honourable place. I am one of their leaders, for their shoes are so high and their heels so short, if they should not be led they'd play domestic tricks abroad and show all.

Petoune Thou, their leader! Why, do they mean to go to the wars?

Antifront I think so, for I am sure here were a couple of gentlemen last night that scoured their pieces.

Petoune I think, Fleer, thy ladies are not very rich.

Antifront How can they? They spend when others get.

Petoune Dost hear, Fleer? Woot prefer me to their service?

Antifront What, shall we embrace? Shall we have red-nosed corporals here? What, you rogue, will you turn sumner? Away, you whale-nosed rogue, away! Go, snuffle, snuffle in the ocean! Away, you slave! [*strikes Petoune*]

Petoune Is thy name Fleer? Th'art a flattering, fleering, cogging knave! Exit

Enter [FELECIA and FLORIDA],
[FELECIA] *singing*

Felecia His man's red hose were the colour of his nose,
And his breech was made of blue,
And he in shape but a French-man's ape,
And so, sweet sir, adieu.
'Holla, holla, ye pampered jades of Asia!
And can you draw but twenty miles a day?'

Florida Give me a bow, I'll hit the sun!

Felecia Why, 'tis impossible.

Florida No more can'st thou hit true felicity.

Felecia Oh, I am in an excellent humour! Now I could laugh, dance, leap, or do any light tricks that belongs to a light wench.

Florida But look, who's here?

Felecia Oh, Signor Fleer, how dost? How dost, man? We may be merry before thee; thou'lt be secret, wo't not?

Antifront As your midwife or barber surgeon, madam.

Felecia How lik'st the city, Fleer? Ha? How lik'st it?

Antifront Faith, well, Madam, were not your citizens such heavy-headed fellows.

Felecia That's a sign they are no drunkards.

Antifront Indeed, madam. Drink lightens the head, the heart, the heels, the pot, the purse; but it makes heavy chamber-pots, full bowels, and foul rooms enough.

Felecia How dost like the gentlemen of this country?

Antifront I can compare your gentleman and your merchant to nothing so fitly as your flea and your louse. I had rather trust your louse with a hundred pound than your flea with forty: for your louse – like the merchant – stands to't, you shall know where to find him, but your flea – like the gentleman – if you take him not at first sight, 'a slips from you.

Florida Methinks they have a strange fashion here, they take money with their wives and give money to their wenches.

Antifront And good reason too, madam! Would you have a man be troubled with a wife, as long as he lives for nothing? 'A gives money to his wench to be as soon rid of her as he has done with her.

Felecia What's the reason, Fleer, the citizens' wives wear all corks in their shoes?

Antifront Oh, madam, to keep the custom of the city only to be light-heeled. The city is like a comedy, both in parts and in apparel, and your gallants are the actors. For he that yesterday played the gentleman now plays the beggar, she that played the waiting-woman now plays the quean, he that played the married man now plays the cuckold, and she that played the lady now plays the painter. Then for their apparel they have change too. For she that wore the petticoat now wears the breech, he that wore the coxcomb now wears the feather, the gentleman that wore the long sword now wears the short hanger, and he that could scarce get velvet for his cape has now lined his cloak throughout with it.

Florida But how dost like the court, Fleer?

Antifront Well enough, if they did not catch their meat so. It comes no sooner from table, but t'one fellow has a fat duck by the rump, th'other a slippery eel by the tail, and an old courtier that best knew the tricks on't was mumbling of a coney in a corner alone by himself.

Felecia What good cheer didst see there?

Antifront Faith, there was much good meat, but

methought your fair lady was your only dish.

Florida Aye, but that's a costly dish and will ask rich saucing.

Antifront Faith, for mine own part, when I had a stomach I should like it best in it own naked kind, without any sauce at all.

Florida What's the news now at court, Fleer?

Antifront Faith, they say your ladies cannot endure the old-fashion spur – they say it hangs to a man's heel like a wheel-barrow – but they love the fine little Scot's spur: it makes the court jennet curvet, curvet gallantly.

Florida I prithee, Fleer, how goes the report of us two abroad?

Antifront If I should tell you, I fear your ladyships would be angry.

Florida No, not a whit.

Antifront But alas, they are your common people. They are like your slippers; they are always gaping, their mouths are never shut.

Florida But what say they of us?

Antifront Alas, Madam, their tongues are like your dry leather shoes, always creaking.

Florida But I prithee tell us, what do they say of us?

Antifront I shall offend your ladyships.

Florida I tell thee, no.

Antifront But alas, madam, I do not believe them, because I know the conditions of the slaves.

Why, I'll tell you, their tongues are like the jack of a clock, still in labour.

Florida I think th'art mad! I prithee tell us what they say.

Antifront I would be loath to displease you.

Florida I tell thee, thou shalt not.

Antifront Faith, they say your ladyships are a couple of stately courtesans.

Florida Faith, that was not much amiss! Said they no worse?

Antifront You'll not be angry with me?

Florida No, o' my word.

Antifront By my troth, they said stately whores.

Florida What pagan rogues be these? Were they but roasted larks for my sake, I would crush 'em bones and all!

Felecia Why are you so angry, sister? You know they speak truth.

Florida Why, are we whores?

Felecia What are we else?

Florida Why, we are courtesans.

Felecia And what difference pray 'e?

Antifront Oh, great, great, madam; your whore is for every rascal, but your courtesan is for your courtier.

Florida [*to* FELECIA] He has given you a difference now.

Antifront And indeed, madam, I said so – for in truth I

was very angry with 'em – but they said you were for every serving-man too.

Florida Did they say so?

Antifront Yes indeed, madam – [*aside*] I hope I have touched you now.

Florida I'll hold my life, this slave the serving-man, that was with me this morning, has bragged of my kindness to him.

Antifront Nay, that's likely, never trust a fellow that will flatter, fleer and fawn for four nobles a year.

Florida Well, I'll ne'er have serving-man touch any linen of mine again.

Antifront Yes, madam, 'a may touch't when 'tis at the laundress's.

Florida Aye, at my laundress's or else not. But what a rascal's this? By this light, I'll never suffer serving-man come near me again.

Antifront Yes, madam, to deliver you a letter or so.

Florida By this hand, not unless the rogue kiss his hand first.

Antifront Oh, madam! Why, since blue coats were left off the kissing of the hand is the serving man's badge, you shall know him by't. But, madam, I speak something boldly of you now and then when I am out of your hearing, to hear what the world will say of you – for you know that's the way to pump filthy words out of their mouths, if there be any in them.

Felecia And do so still; we allow thee to say anything, for thereby we shall know our friends from our foes.

Antifront I assure your ladyships, I love you and am sorry for you from my soul, although you know it not.

Florida We doubt it not.

Felecia Come, sister, will you in?

Florida I prithee, Fleer, inform us how the tide of opinion runs on us, lest we be drowned in the slanderous imaginations of the world.

Antifront I shall be very vigilant of your reputations.

Both Be so. *Exeunt* [FLORIDA *and* FELECIA]

Enter RUFFLE [*in fine clothes*]

Antifront Who comes here, a' God's name? Oh, my gallant ruffles it out in silk! Where have you been all this while?

Ruffle Faith, at court, Fleer. When wert thou there?

Antifront Faith, but yesterday, where I saw a farmer's son sit newly made a courtier, that sat in the presence at cards as familiar as if the chair of state had been made of a piece of his father's barn door. Oh, 'tis a shame: I would have state be state in earnest and in game. I like your courtier for nothing but often saying his prayers.

Ruffle What, I think thou seldom sayst thy prayers, since thou hast almost forgot thy paternoster.

Antifront Faith, I pray once a week; dost thou pray

oftener?

Ruffle I did pray oftener when I was an Englishman but I have not prayed often, I must confess, since I was a Briton. But dost hear, Fleer? Canst tell me if an Englishman were in debt, whether a Briton must pay it or no?

Antifront No, questionless no.

Ruffle I'm glad of that; I hope some honest statute will come shortly and wipe out all my scores.

Antifront But what's the news now abroad, Master Ruffle?

Ruffle Why, they say the courtiers shall make the citizens no more cuckolds.

Antifront Excellent news, i'faith, excellent news! Then the court will grow rich.

Ruffle Rich? Why, man, why?

Antifront Why, then your courtier will not bestow his money in buying the merchant's idle commodities to lie with his wife.

Ruffle Fleer, I did but to try thee; the tide of the flood is turned, man.

Antifront Then let them sweat for't.

Ruffle For what?

Antifront If they strive against the stream.

Ruffle No, but I mean the citizens must cuckold the courtiers.

Antifront Excellent news, i'faith, excellent news! Then the court will grow rich.

Ruffle What, like your weaver's shuttle? Make cloth

forward and backward? But how, I prithee? But hark you, Fleer, are you capable of a secret?

Antifront As your common cockatrice that receives the secrets of every man.

Ruffle Then I must entreat I may trust thee.

Antifront That's because I am no tailor, for if I were thou would'st entreat me to trust thee.

Ruffle Sirrah, they say your ladies are a couple of common punks. I hope I may trust you with a secret –

Antifront Sir, sir, do y'hear? Do y'think they are no worse?

Ruffle Worse! Why, can they be worse?

Antifront Oh, sir, aye, they may be private punks. Why, I tell you, he that takes up his private punk's linen were better take up any commodity about the town; if 'twere a commodity of mouse-traps 'a should not lose much by the bargain.

Ruffle But hark you, Fleer, hark you: 'tis supposed – I can tell you – they are a couple of private punks.

Antifront Nay, then there's some hope they'll prove honest women.

Ruffle Yea? How, Fleer, how?

Antifront Why, your private punk would leave being a punk rather than be private to one man for nothing. And then if all men were like thee they would be honest, for thou hast nothing to give 'em.

Ruffle [*aside*] What a cogging, fleering rogue is this? Nothing will anger him! [*to* ANTIFRONT] But do y'hear, Fleer, art thou a procurer or a knave? For one of them I am sure thou art.

Antifront A procurer? What's that?

Ruffle One that procures means for procreation, vulgarly called a pander.

Antifront By this light, now, were I a notable rogue should I deny my profession! Why, I am a procurer, sir.

Ruffle Nay, then thou art a knave too, that's certain, for there is such a sympathy between a procurer and a knave as there is betwixt an alchemist and a beggar.

Antifront But, look you sir, pray 'e, will you tell me one thing now?

Ruffle What's that?

Antifront Are you a whore-master or a thief? For one of them I'm sure you are.

Ruffle [*aside*] By this light, now 'a comes near me too! [*to* ANTIFRONT] Why, I am a whore-master.

Antifront Nay, then you are a thief too, that's certain, for your whore-master always filcheth for victuals, for you know flesh is man's food. Marry, sir, you cannot be hanged for't, 'tis but petty larceny at most, but you may chance be whipped for't and burned too – but not i'th' hand, Signor, not i'th' hand.

Enter SPARK

Spark Save ye, gentles.

Ruffle Then we are enemies to the Jews.

Antifront Oh, my good preferer! How does your worship? You are a stranger here.

Spark Faith, I have been with two gentlewomen in whose company thou first saw'st us. And there the knight, Sir John Have-Little, is so in love with the younger as 'a knows not whether 'a should rejoice she had so much beauty or lament because he is like to enjoy none on't.

Antifront By my troth, I took him for a conjurer when I first saw him, 'a talked so much of his soul and the devil.

Spark Why, 'a sold his soul to the devil, man, for the velvet that lines his cloak.

Antifront And when will he give the devil his due?

Spark Nay, 'a deals with him as 'a does with his tailor: goes upon trust and means to pay them both at the latter day.

Antifront But does not the gentlewomen jest at him?

Spark Yes. One of them asked if he were a celestrial or a terrestrial knight and he very ignorantly asked what knights they were. 'Your terrestrial knight', quoth she, 'is of a gross element and lives upon lands of his own, but your celestrial knight he lives by the heir, that is, by his elder brother. He it was, was knighted when so few 'scaped the sword, and he it is that now lives by the sword.'

Antifront And what said the knight? What said he?

Spark Faith, as some courtiers do: laugh at that he did not understand and swore an oath or two of the new fashion, as 'by my conscience, lady, you have a very good spirit'. And so after two or three court-compliments beseeched the ladies retain him still in their good graces, kissed his hand and went his way.

Antifront Faith, methinks your English ladies were very gallant creatures had they not one fault.

Spark What's that?

Antifront I have heard say they will rise sooner and go with more devotion to see an extraordinary execution than to hear a sermon.

Spark O Signor, condemn not all for some; indeed I must confess there have been ladies at executions.

Antifront Aye, and they sat bare-faced too, for fear the little fleet holes of their masks should not give their eyes room enough for such a prospect. One lady thrust her head so far out at a window, with greedy desire to see all, that the whole body was like to follow, making a forked tree with her head down, had not her gentleman usher – contrary to the nature of his office – catched hold of her behind.

Spark A forked tree? Why, what tree dost thou think she would have made?

Antifront Oh, sir, a medlar tree, a medlar tree.

Spark But Fleer, how does the gentleman usher live with thy ladies?

Antifront Faith, sir, in the nature of a monkey that flatters and fawns, and shakes his tail in his mistress's lap. But i'faith, gallants, whither are you two bound now?

Spark We are even ready for your two ladies, Signor.

Antifront Faith, and you shall find my two ladies as ready for you two. Come, come, I'll put you in the way of all flesh: I'll send you to Gravesend, I'll see you in the tilt-boat. When you are there, ship yourselves in: in, in.

[*Exeunt* SPARK and RUFFLE]

Enter PISO *and* [HAVE-LITTLE]

Piso How is't, Fleer?

Antifront Oh, my lord, you are a welcome man.

Have-Little Save you, O Signor.

Antifront Oh, my gracious knight, and whither are you two bound now?

Piso Faith, e'en to your two ladies, Signor.

Antifront Yea? And will you to the southward, i'faith? Will you to the confines of Italy, my gallants? Take heed how ye go northwards: 'tis a dangerous coast, jest not with't in winter; therefore go southwards, my gallants, southwards ho! I have shipped two gallants in a storm; I fear they have spent their main masts by this time and are coming home again. But if you will southwards, my hearts of gold,

I'll ship you in pomp; I'll send ye under the very line where the sun's at hottest.

Piso But come, shall we go see thy ladies, Fleer?

Antifront Aye, aye, aye, come. But, my good lord, you'll be a welcome man, for I have heard her often swear that had she such a husband – a man so richly decked in virtuous ornaments – she would forsake this life, herself, nay, her very being, to be yours. Oh, my good lord, she loves you dearly.

Piso Phew! But I cannot requite it.

Antifront Why, my good lord?

Piso She's a common thing.

Antifront But say she may turn, my lord.

Piso She has been so much worn, she's not worth the turning now.

Antifront O my lord, penitence doth purge a spotted soul and better leave sin late than not at all. And I do know, my lord, that for your love from her immodest life she'll turn.

Piso Aye, aye, I doubt not but she'll turn, but 'twill be like a buzzard hawk that turns tail to her game.

Have-Little Fleer, is the gentleman usher that I preferred to your ladies in any favour with them?

Antifront Great, great: 'a kisses his hand with an excellent grace and 'a will leer and fleer upon 'em. He's partly their physician: 'a makes 'em suppositories and gives 'em glisters.

Have-Little And how lives he with 'em?

Antifront Faith, like Thisbe in the play – 'a has almost killed himself with the scabbard. But hark you, knight, you'll be a welcome man to my younger lady; I protest she thinks worthily of you.

Have-Little Signor, I must confess I am beholding to your lady and – to tell you truly – I have much affected her since I first saw her.

Antifront Upon my word, sir, to my knowledge she is an honest gentlewoman; yet the world may chance speak ill of her. Why, I have heard some say Penelope was a punk, having no reason to suspect her but because she sat up late a-nights, when 'twas but to undo that which she did by day. I have heard some say Hercules was a coward because he did not fight at single rapier like a gallant, but with a club.

Have-Little Nay, I have no reason to think the worse of her for the report of the world; for the world, Signor, perchance speaks ill of you or me.

Antifront Why, y'are in th' right: I have heard some say you were a very needy knight and that you had but one shirt to your back when you came first to this town. Nay, more: when your lackey carried it to the laundress it was found to be a woman's smock that you had borrowed. But what? Should my lady or I believe this now?

Have-Little I hope she doth not.

Antifront No, no, no.

Piso Come, Fleer, shall we see thy ladies?

Antifront Aye, aye. Ho! Who's within there?

Enter SERVING-MAN

Serving-man What would you have, Master Fleer?

Antifront Prithee show these gentlemen up into the great chamber and give my ladies notice of their being there. [*to* PISO *and* HAVE-LITTLE] Have a little business my lords; he'll conduct ye, ye shall find a couple of your acquaintance there.

Exeunt [SERVING-MAN, PISO *and* HAVE-LITTLE; ANTIFRONT *remains*]

Could I but work Lord Piso and my eldest daughter to make 'em both affect and love each other, that marriage might unite their hearts together! Oh, then there were assured hope we might redeem our honours lost and regain our right in Florence. And for this knight, though he be poor yet would he married were unto Felecia.
For oft a loving husband's awful eye
Sets right the woman's steps that went awry.
Heaven I know has grace enough in store,
To make most chaste a most lascivious whore.

Enter [NAN and SUSAN] *in boys' apparel*

How now? Who have we here? A couple of footmen?

Susan You see, sir, we are not a-horseback.

Antifront How now, my little fireworks of wit? What,

flashes and flames? Tell me true, were you never ushers to some great man's coach-mares? Did you never run bare before them?

Nan Never we, sir.

Antifront Whither are you going?

Susan Sir, we want a service and are going to get a master.

Antifront Come, come, I'll prefer you both. Thou shalt serve a countryman of mine – he's going to travel, shalt go with him – and thou shalt serve one of my ladies.

Susan We would willingly serve two near friends because we are brothers and indeed two twins, and therefore are loath to be parted.

Antifront Two twins? That's all one; come, come, you shall serve 'em.

Nan You shall pardon us, sir.

Enter FLORIDA, SPARK, FELECIA, RUFFLE, PISO, [HAVE-LITTLE] *and* FROMAGA

Florida [*to* SPARK] I hope you'll not condemn me for my love.

Spark I have no reason, lady.

Florida I offered you unasked.

Spark That which a number oft hath bought.

Florida Partly they have and partly not, for I would have you know my function seldom sells affection. What though I have evil lived?

Repentant tears can wash away my sin, which I'll pour forth like drops of winter rain, and now henceforth ever I'll this life abhor and to the earth my knees I'll daily bow to get mercy from heaven, love from you.

Nan [*aside*] Oh, the devil take impudency! She courts him!

Spark Madam, the love that I may give you, fully do enjoy; but I have sworn with other love than as a brother doth a sister never to love any.

Felecia [*to* RUFFLE] O sir, my fortunes are not fellows with my birth, they make me stoop to base dejected courses; but would you love me, I would as swift as thought fly this life and leave lust's foulest sin for fleshly beasts to sleep and wallow in.

Susan [*aside*] Shame to thy sex, no more!

Ruffle Lady, in all the honest offices that friendship may command, command me still. But yet I have not seen the face to which I owe so much of love as may justly arrest my affections, and when I do I'll pay so due a debt without imprisonment.

Piso [*aside*] Methinks yond' lady grows fairer much than she was wont; methinks her feature mends, and her comely gesture much hath drawn my heart to love her – oh, but she's a whore!

Nan [*to* SPARK *and* RUFFLE] Gentlemen, do you lack a boy?

Spark No.

Nan O God, I am undone.

Susan [*to* RUFFLE] Sir, do y'want a servant?

Ruffle No.

Susan O Lord, what shall I do?

Piso [*to* NAN] What canst do?

Nan Anything that a boy should do.

Have-Little [*to* SUSAN] Woot dwell with me?

Susan 'Tis partly as you'll use me.

Have-Little I'll use thee well.

Susan Well.

Piso [*to* SUSAN *and* NAN] Tell me, are you both content to dwell with us two?

Both As please you two.

Piso [*to* NAN] Then thou shalt live with me.

Have-Little [*to* SUSAN] And thou with me.

Spark [*to* PISO *and* HAVE-LITTLE] Come, gentlemen, will you be going?

Both We attend you, sir.

Spark Ladies, our occasions calls us hence and I am sorry we must leave you.

Florida Gentlemen, you all both have and ever shall be welcome.

Exeunt [RUFFLE, SPARK, HAVE-LITTLE *and* SUSAN]*;* [FLORIDA, FELECIA], PISO, NAN [*and* ANTIFRONT *remain*]

Piso [*to* FLORIDA] Lady, I will leave you much affection more than I thought to lend you, but I deal on use and have much interest.

Antifront [*aside*] Caught, I hope: hold hook and line – he's fast, by heaven!

Florida My lord, what you lend me with much interest shall be repaid.

Piso Adieu.

Florida Fare you well.

[*Exeunt* PISO, NAN *and* ANTIFRONT]

[*to* FELECIA] Refused!

Felecia Contemned!

Florida Disdained!

Felecia Abused!

Florida 'A dies.

Felecia 'A shall not live.

Florida Disdain the daughter of such a Signor?

Felecia Contemn a lady born? Sister, we are wronged.

Florida But, if you'll consent, I have a project laid that in requital both of them shall die.

Felecia You make my soul sweet harmony. Come, let's about it then. *Exeunt*

[Act 3, Scene 1]

Enter [FELECIA *and* FLORIDA] *each with a letter, and* [ANTIFRONT] *aside*

Florida Are we in private?

Felecia We are.

Florida Pray, sister, what moving lines of love has your knight touched your affection with?

Felecia Faith, his style is plain; only a little court-like silken phrase it has. But I hope your lord hath sent rich words like jewels for your ears against your nuptial day?

Florida Faith, 'a woos with lines that might persuade another, though not me, which I'll lend your eyes upon the like received courtesy from you.

Felecia With all my heart. [*They exchange letters*]

Florida What have we here? [*Reads*] 'Lady, I know the nobleness of your disposition defends you from the least spark of baseness, wherefore I invocate every particular virtue of yours to be mediators to your best judgement for my better estimation in your love. My affection is zealous; my intent honourable; my desire, marriage. Thus, desiring your resolved answers, I rest ever at your disposure, Jack Have-Little, Knight.' [*to* FELECIA] Upon my life, some friend did pen it for the fool.

Felecia Let me see, what's this? [*Reads*] 'You, the

understanding spirit of a woman, let the splendour of your beauty, with some heat of your affection, shine upon the creature that adores ye, and with the heavenly comfort of your love, melt and thaw despair from my dying heart. Which if it live, it lives to love; if die, it dies in love. But, howsoever, 'tis yours: 'twas made for you, lives by you and dies without you. Yours in the most zealous degree of affection, Don Piso de Florence.' [*to* FLORIDA] Sister, upon my life this is son and heir to Duke Piso that now is.

Florida Oh, would he were! But whoso'er he be, 'a must be made a match to give fire to the hell-black powder of our revenge. Yet your love – the wise knight – and he are two in one, there are no such friends as they.

Felecia Then let them march both hand-in-hand in one way.

Florida Then shall be thus: these two being earnest suitors for our loves, we'll grant upon condition that suddenly they murder Spark and Ruffle. But first to take the sacrament if ever it be known – as known 'twill be – to keep our names unspotted in the action. This being done –

Felecia Let them challenge us, we and our loves are won. But say they should reveal us?

Florida Oh, none will break a sacrament to heap up perjury on other sins when death and hell stands gaping for their souls.

Felecia But say they rail on us?

Florida If they do, 'tis known we loved Spark and Ruffle, and men will think they killed 'em for our loves, since they lived in our favour, these in disgrace.

Felecia I like it well; come, let's hasten it.
For this is e'en as true as e'er was text,
Plots are but dreams until they take effects.

Exeunt [FLORIDA *and* FELECIA]

Antifront O God, I think the path to hell that women tread is broader than the way men go; how they walk by couples to the devil!

Enter PISO

Piso Oh, that I should love a whore, a very common cockatrice! My thoughts are drowned in a gulf of sin. She's a very cannibal which doth devour man's flesh, and a horseleech that sucks out men's best blood's perfection; a very prisoner's box that's ope' for every man's benevolence. And I am heir unto a duke, yet love her. Doth any man here love a whore? Aye. Who? Aye, aye, aye: 'tis I. An arrant punk and common hired hackney, and yet I love her, I adore her, I dote on her, I worship her! Oh, would some good man would cut my throat and put me out of pain – of pain! Oh, that nature would not make an honest woman!

Antifront She did, she did, my lord.

Piso Art there? Speak, who wast?

Antifront Eve, Eve, my lord, she was honest.

Piso Art sure on't?

Antifront Aye, sure, my lord, for there was no man to tempt her but her husband.

Piso I thought 'twas some such country gentlewoman. O Fleer, Fleer, I love a whore!

Antifront Why, my lord, were you never a soldier?

Piso Yes, yes.

Antifront Why, then, 'tis your profession; you need not be ashamed of your trade.

Piso But Fleer, woot help me? Woot help me, man?

Antifront Aye, aye. Who is't?

Piso Thy lady, thy elder lady.

Antifront Oh, my lord, love her? Why, she's a whore!

Piso Aye, Fleer, but she may turn.

Antifront But she is so much worn, my lord, she's not worth turning now.

Piso Do not vex me, do not torment me, do not torture me upon the rack of jests! I tell thee, if she please she may turn.

Antifront Aye, my lord; tail to her game like a buzzard hawk, or so.

Piso Yet again! Now the devil take thy body and damnation light upon thy soul, destruction on thy bones, confusion in thy marrow! Dost scorn me, mock me, vex me, torment me? Dost? Dost? I'll hang myself – nay, I'll damn myself rather than love thy lady and be abused by thee! I will, I will! *Exit* PISO

Enter [HAVE-LITTLE]

Have-Little O Fleer, how dost thy lady?

Antifront I delivered your letter, sir, and she thanks you for't.

Have-Little And how does she, ha? How does she?

Antifront Faith, not well. She has taken physic, and your gentleman usher there ministers to her; she's very great, and she says she feels much stirring in her belly.

Have-Little Sure then, Fleer, she has eaten too much raw fruit.

Antifront Upon my life then, they be plums and the stones make her swell.

Have-Little Sure, then, 'tis so. I should send her something to comfort her now being sick. What dost think were best, Fleer?

Antifront Send her an oaten cake, 'tis a good northern token. Sir Ralph Shave sent his mistress one, but I think 'a meant to ride a journey on her and thought oats would make her travel well.

Have-Little No, oats is too great a binder after her physic. I care not if I go and visit her and carry her a woodcock.

Antifront You'll go alone, sir.

Have-Little Aye, I mean so; but how should I carry him, Fleer?

Antifront Under your cloak, sir, under your cloak.

Have-Little Mass, and thou sayest true; I'll go buy one

straight. And yet, now I remember me, 'tis no great matter if I defer it till she be well: it shall be so, Fleer, I will.

Antifront Oh, y'are of a French humour, sir, as inconstant as impatient; I think you have scarce the patience to tell the clock when it strikes.

Have-Little Tush, I keep a boy for such uses.

Antifront For nothing else?

Have-Little Yes, to wear a guarded cloak.

Antifront Not till you be richly married.

Have-Little No, not till I be richly married; he should wear one now if my money were come out o'th' country.

Antifront I wonder you would be knighted, sir, since your money is so long a-coming that you cannot maintain your knighthood gallantly.

Have-Little Faith, I was knighted to get me a good wife, Fleer.

Antifront Get you a good wife? Why, look you, sir, speak but the golden tongue very perfectly – marry, you must speak it well, and call some great lord cousin – 'twill get you a better wife than three hundred pound jointure. You may report you have coal-pits too; 'tis a warm commodity I can tell you. They may be sent about by water; if they ne'er come – as your money doth not – you may curse the winds or complain of shipwreck and then, though't be a lie, 'tis drowned.

Have-Little Aye, but say it should be proved afterwards 'twas not true?

Antifront True? God's my life, she's a wise woman that will go as far as Newcastle to search the depth of a coal-pit for your truth!

Have-Little I would be loath to leave my truth so far hence.

Antifront [*aside*] But I am sure he'll bring his honesty no nearer hither; but that comes about by water, too, as his money does.

Have-Little But, Fleer, is not thy lady a virtuous gentlewoman?

Antifront Oh yes, sir, I often find her in deep contemplation.

Have-Little Of what, I prithee?

Antifront Of Aretino's pictures.

Have-Little Aye, I warrant her. Oh, she can endure no bawdry; she spits when she hears one speak on't.

Antifront That's because her mouth waters at it.

Have-Little She's wondrous musical too.

Antifront Very true, she every day sings 'John for the King' and at 'Up Tails All' she's perfect.

Have-Little Be these good tunes, Fleer?

Antifront Excellent, excellent, sir – far better than your Scottish jigs.

Have-Little Yet many of our ladies delight much in the Scottish music.

Antifront Aye, with their instruments.

Have-Little Thou hast a good wit, Fleer: if I were a great man thou should'st be my secretary.

Antifront And I hope I should discharge the place sufficiently, for I have learning enough to take a bribe and wit enough to be proud. But whither are you going now, sir?

Have-Little Faith, I am going to thy ladies, Fleer.

Antifront You will not speak with 'em now, for my ladies will speak with none but gentlemen.

Have-Little Why, sir, I hope I am a knight, and knights are before gentlemen.

Antifront What, knights before gentlemen, say ye?

Have-Little Faith, aye.

Antifront That's strange, they were wont to be gentlemen 'fore they were knighted; but for this news I'll follow you.

Have-Little Do, and as occasion serves I'll prefer thee. *Exeunt*

[3.2]

Enter PISO*, and* NAN *as his boy*

Piso Why should I love her? Because she's fair. Because she's fair; because she's a whore – for if she were not fair she would not be a whore, and if she were not fair I should not love her. Ergo, if she were not a whore I should not love her. Well concluded, wit! Well concluded, wit: there is no man breathing could love her but I. She's a whore yet her beauty haunts me like a ghost, I cannot sleep for't; her remembrance rides me like the mare a-nights, I cannot rest for't. What shall I do? I shall burst! [*to* NAN] Boy!

Nan My lord.

Piso Will thy tongue be secret?

Nan As the clapper of a mill, my lord.

Piso Is not that always going?

Nan Aye, my lord, but I hope it says nothing.

Piso Oh, thou hast wit, I see! I am in love, boy. I am, I am.

Nan With whom, my lord?

Piso With a very wagtail, an arrant woman, a very peacock whose pride is maintained by her tail.

Nan Then it is maintained by the worthiest part of her body.

Piso Come, your wit, boy, your proof.

Nan If a hundred men in a company meet, doth not the worthiest man amongst them first take his place and sit down?

Piso I grant it.

Nan And I am sure, my lord, where'er the body comes the tail first takes his place and sits down, and therefore I hope 'tis the worthiest part of the body.

Piso Oh, that I had the reason of a sailor to know her like a rock, that I might sail from her and avoid her! Or as a virtuous man knows sin, to loath and leave it. And yet she's wondrous fair; I would she were as honest. Kind usage may reclaim her from her sin, and make her stoop unto her husband's will as doth a well-manned hawk unto the lure.

Nan Oh, aye, she has been manned already; she knows the lure and will come to any call.

Piso Oh, but her beauty may excuse the folly of her youth! 'Tis want of maintenance hath overthrown her; want and pride are two notorious bawds: want makes the noblest creature sell her soul for gold and pride doth make the gallants stoop to lust.

Nan And often sells pure honesty to clad her tail in glittering bravery.

Piso And 'tis well done; let every member wear that which it won. Why should the head study to maintain the foot?

Nan Or the foot trot to maintain the head?

Piso Why should not every member, like a mechanic man in a commonwealth, labour in his own trade to maintain itself? Then since everything must live, I will no more condemn beauty for being clad in luxury, but henceforth I will love her and let my passion smoothly swim along the stream of love's affection. Henceforth I will no more with foul and hated thoughts abuse so rare a creature, whose behaviour and discourse enchants the ears of men and drives the world into a wonder! [*Sighs*] Ay me!

Nan Faith, my lord, you'll ne'er win a woman by sighing, crossing your arms and crying 'ay me'! The only way to win them is to care little for 'em. When they are sad, do ye sing; when they sing and are merry, then take your time and put 'em to't. If they will, so; if not, let them snick up! If you will walk in, my lord, I'll show ye many principles I learned of my mother; they may do your lordship good.

Piso Go, go, I will. But oh, unhappy fate,
When youth and weakness must support our state!

Exeunt

[3.3] *Enter* [ANTIFRONT] *one way,* SPARK, RUFFLE *and* PETOUNE *another way*

Spark How now, Fleer?

Ruffle Save you, Fleer.

Antifront Save ye, gallants. [*to* PETOUNE] O Signor Petoune, shall you and I be friends again?

Spark Why, are ye enemies?

Antifront No great enemies: a quarrel rose between us.

Petoune I do not like such quarrels. 'A struck me, sir, and I protest and swear to you, sir, by this trinidado, had I not taken the box on my cheek, 'a had broke my pipe.

Spark [*to* ANTIFRONT] Why didst not strike him again?

Ruffle Oh no, his father's a Justice.

Antifront Nay, if the father be of the peace I see no reason the son should fight.

Ruffle What, a coward, Signor? Fie! A coward?

Antifront A coward? Why, that's his only virtue, for a coward abuseth no man but 'a makes him satisfaction. For if 'a wrong all men, 'a gives all men leave to beat him. He's like a whetstone: he sets an edge on another and yet 'a will not cut himself.

Ruffle Come, come, we must needs have you friends and thou'st do him some good offices.

Antifront Who, I? With all my heart! But what is't, sir? What is't?

Ruffle Thou shalt commend his love to Madam Fromaga.

Antifront His love to her? What, Signor, in love with my lady's ancient?

Spark Why her ancient?

Antifront Because she carries her colours for her but 'tis in a box. But, Signor, you shall have a good match on't: though she be not rich yet she's an ancient woman and is able to get her living by midwifery. And I can tell ye, 'tis not the worst trade going, considering how young and old and all do their good wills to set them a-work. And 'tis a good hearing. Better they get than the lawyers, for your midwives live by the agreement between party and party and the falling-in of lovers, but the lawyers live by the falling-out of friends.

Petoune I pray, sir, what may she be worth?

Antifront Worth? Let me see: she hath three yellow periwigs of her own, she hath a fan with a short silver handle, about the length of a barber's syringe, she has a looking-glass too – but that has played the prodigal citizen with her, 'tis broken – and much other goods of the same nature.

Spark But come, Signor, how will you woo her?

Petoune I will tell her she is so wise that neither age nor time could cozen her of beauty.

Antifront And, by my faith, that will do well.

Petoune I will tell her that I love her most for the whiteness of her skin.

Antifront But you may not say the sweetness of her breath, for that stinks.

Petoune I will praise the smallness of her fingers.

Antifront But I assure you, you may better praise the length of her nails.

Petoune I am afraid that being old she has a dry hand.

Antifront That's certain, but she has a very moist nose, you may praise her for that. But, my gallants, why are ye such strangers at our little court?

Spark Because thy ladies live like the beadles of Bridewell.

Antifront How's that, sir?

Spark By the sins of the people.

Ruffle They say the Lord Piso hath been a good client to thy elder lady of late.

Antifront The more fool he! Why your good client is but like your study-gown – sits in the cold himself to keep the lawyer warm.

Spark And what fees hast thou out of their trade?

Antifront Faith, my fees are like a puny clerk's, a penny a sheet.

Spark How a penny a sheet?

Antifront Why, if any lie with them a whole night I make the bed i'th' morning, and for that I have two pence and that's a penny a sheet.

Ruffle What gallants use to come to your house?

Antifront All sorts, all nations and all trades. There is first Master Gallant your Briton, Master Metheglins your Welshman, Monsieur Mushroom the Frenchman, Señor Fumada the Spaniard, Master Usquebaugh the Irishman and Master Shamrock his lackey. Oh, and Master Slopdragon the Dutchman. Then for your tradesmen, there comes first Master Saluberrimum the physician, Master Smooth the silk-man, Master Thimble the tailor, Master Blade the cutler and Master Rowel the spurrier. But Master Match the gunner of Tower Hill comes often. He has taught my ladies to make fireworks: they can deal in chambers already as well as all the gunners that make 'em fly off with a train at Lambeth when the Mayor and Aldermen land at Westminster.
[*to* PETOUNE] But come, Signor, you have tobacco and I'll give you a cup of mulled sack, and we'll e'en go drink a health to our mistresses. *Exeunt*

[Act 4, Scene 1]

Enter [FLORIDA, FELECIA,] PISO, HAVE-LITTLE, *and* FROMAGA *one way:* SPARK, RUFFLE, PETOUNE *and* [ANTIFRONT] *another way*

Florida Health to our best esteemed friends, Master Spark and Master Ruffle.

Felecia Our good wishes ever wait upon our best beloved friends, Master Ruffle and Master Spark.

Both We both are much indebted to your ladyships.

Antifront [*to* PETOUNE] Look ye, Signor, that's she whose love means to assault your brains, since you have blown up your own sconce with tobacco.

Petoune As I am truly generous, she's modest. [*to* FROMAGA] Fair mistress, you are so wise that neither time nor age could ever cozen you of beauty. And I swear even by the Alps' high heaven-touching tops, the traveller's narrow passage and by the towering head of high mount Chiego, the seaman's southward mark; by these the witnesses unto my travel I do vow that you are passing fair.

Fromaga If I be not fair, sir, I must be foul.

Petoune A fowl lady? What bird might that be?

Fromaga A foul lady? Y'are a saucy jack to call me so, that you are.

Petoune Oh be not angry, for I protest I cannot but commend the whiteness of your skin.

Fromaga Marry, muff! I think 'a be a tanner and means to buy me for my skin.

Petoune [*to* ANTIFRONT] God's me, she's angry! What shall I do now, Signor?

Antifront To her again, man! Do not leave her: the moon is now upon change, she will turn.

Petoune [*to* FROMAGA] I pray you, lady, know me by the title of some kindness.

Fromaga Kindness? Faith, sir, you are mistaken in me; you must seek your flirts some other where, and, I pray, come not to make a fool of me! Alas, man, though I am a waiting-woman, do not think I spend my time in nothing but tempering of colours, working of drawn-work, warming of smocks and pinning in of ruffs. Faith, yes.

Antifront And you come to her, Signor. You must come to her as country gentlewomen do into the fashion: that is, in the tail and latter end on't.

Fromaga Faith, aye! And ye come to begin your knavery on me, I'll take you down! I am none of your young simpering waiting-women that are ashamed to be counted proud and therefore suffer every serving-man to use them at their pleasure.

Petoune Now on my conscience, mistress, my love is honest and I desire marriage.

Fromaga Indeed, if you mean marriage I am content to bear the more with you. But I pray 'e, sir, when shall we be married? By my troth, I ask you because I have been so often deceived; I warrant you, I have been promised and dealt upon promises in the way of marriage above an hundred times.

Petoune At our next meeting we will set down a day for the effecting of it.

Florida [*to* SPARK *and* RUFFLE] Gentlemen, we have some small discourse which a little requires secrecy, therefore if it please ye to walk in and make use of our better rooms we will not long be absent from you.

Both With all our hearts.

Exeunt [SPARK, RUFFLE, PETOUNE *and* FROMAGA;] [FLORIDA, FELECIA, PISO *and* HAVE-LITTLE *remain;* ANTIFRONT, NAN *and* SUSAN] *hide themselves*

Florida [*to* PISO] Worthy lord, do not think immodesty in me, though, contrary to the bashful habit of my sex, I am enforced by love's almighty power to reveal the secrets of my heart. Your letters have so much prevailed with me that in a word I must confess – I love you.

Felecia [*to* HAVE-LITTLE] Worthy knight, I would my words had but the power to work in you that which your lines have done in me! Then should the happy consolation of my life dwell ever in your love's embracements.

Have-Little [*to* FELECIA] Assure ye, lady, your gift of love to me shall be deserved, though nothing but my life's dear breath requite it.

Piso [*to* FLORIDA] And I will rather die a shameful death than live a hateful life, which I must do unless I find a means that may deserve your love.

Florida Now your tongue goes like a well-tuned instrument and makes my heart within my bosom dance with joy to hear such large requital of my love! But durst you, to maintain this your affection, although it were with some danger of your life –

Piso Durst I? I vow even by my soul's eternity I durst.

Florida Alas, if you knew all! 'Tis your own good, not mine; and yet I lie, 'tis my good too, since my life depends upon your safety.

Piso What is't, dear lady? Although it be the death of man, if it be pleasing unto you I'll do't.

Florida Oh, let me embrace so dear a spirit in so dear a bosom! And, since you have bound yourself by promise, I will be plain. There are two that hate you two, because we love you, and often have persuaded us by gifts and large protestations to have us love them if they killed you.

Piso What, us?

Have-Little Who, we?

Florida Nay, 'tis too true. For while you lived, they said there was no hope for them to look for any love from us. Now, we poor silly women, fearing lest they without consent of us should do that which their hatred doth intend, we think it fit prevention first be used by giving them to drink of what themselves have brewed.

Piso First murder them.

Felecia True. So shall ye then be sure t'enjoy our loves, we yours, and live secure.

Piso But what are they, ladies?

Florida Spark –

Felecia And Ruffle.

Piso They die for't, though they were my father's sons.

Have-Little They shall not live.

Piso Let little children fear the shallow brooks, for I can swim though't be through seas of blood; let foolish fear go dwell with women, for bloody resolution shall not part from me. I'll kill them both, even with mine own hands I'll do't.

Florida Oh no, I'll reveal it then! Unless you first do swear and take a sacrament, whatever hap to keep our names untouched.

Piso Untouched? We'll do't.

Felecia Then for the means –

Have-Little We'll stab them!

Piso We'll fight with them!

Florida No, so you may miss them and they kill you.

Felecia Give them a fig!

Florida Make them drink their last!

Felecia Poison them!

Piso But for the means –

Florida You two shall make a banquet, and in a cup of wine a health shall pass –

Piso In which I'll mingle such a dram, as they shall ride to heaven in post unless they miss the way.

Have-Little But where shall we get the poison? Because you know 'tis dangerous, and will breed suspect where e'er we buy it.

Piso I have a countryman in town, an apothecary – one Signor Alunio – a fellow that is well stored and will sell me of the best.

Nan [*aside*] If 'a were of my mind, 'a would think no poison too good for you.

Florida Come then, I would have you go about the preparation of the feast.

Exeunt [FLORIDA, FELECIA, PISO *and* HAVE-LITTLE]

Antifront Now, boys, you have a couple of goodly masters.

Nan Aye, Fleer, and thou hast a couple of virtuous mistresses. Oh, they are a couple of damned pieces that will plot or counsel the death of two such worthy gentlemen!

Susan For one of them the earth did never bear a worthier creature.

Nan Which is that?

Susan Which is that? Why, sister, have you so oft confessed that his all-perfectioned spirit points him out for virtue herself to imitate, and yet do y'ask now which is that?

Antifront How? Sister? Nay, now I smell you, i'faith! Do y'hear, do y'hear? Whose fiddlers are you two? What instruments do you bear, I pray?

Nan You have told a wise tale! Faith, sir, we carry none.

Antifront 'Tis true, my little musicians; you carry but the cases, my little curtals. I'faith, I smell a smock here too! And are you two wenches, i'faith?

Nan If we were, I hope thou would'st not wrong us.

Antifront No, as I am true Italian born.

Susan Then, 'tis true, we confess to thee: we are both wenches and the love of these two gentlemen – Spark and Ruffle – hath made us leave ourselves to wait on them, which by misfortune we did miss.

Antifront But believe me, my little gallants, ye play the boys well.

Nan Well? Why, I'll tell thee, I have played the boy so long as I am changed into the nature of a boy! I'll go to span-counter with any page in Europe for his best garters. I can tell bawdy tales, drink drunk, brag, swear, and lie with any lackey in the town.

Susan I can man a punk to a play or slander any gentlewoman as well as any Inns o' Court puny.

I can as well as he swear such a lady is in love with me and such a citizen's daughter would have come to bed to me, when all shall be as true as thy ladies are honest.

Nan I wonder thou'lt live in such a sinful place.

Susan Thy ladies are as common as any tavern door.

Antifront Good comparisons, for a man comes no sooner into a tavern but he's welcome, and the operation of the pot makes him not able to stand when he comes out.

Nan But what shall we do in this matter?

Susan Do? Why, complain them to the magistrates and prevent the murder!

Antifront No, not so. I'll tell you how't shall be, hark in your ears. [*whispers*]

Both Do it and we shall ever thank thee.

Antifront Come, let's about it then. *Exeunt*

[4.2]

Enter Signor ALUNIO *the apothecary in his shop with wares about him*

Alunio What's this? Oh, this is eryngo: this makes the old man able and the young man lusty, strengtheneth the nerves and doth concoct the blood, and her name is written on the box because my wife should know it in my absence. This is civet, this comes from the cat's tail; I would my wife were such a cat. This perfumes your ladies, and not without cause for some – I mean, whose sweet breath is dead and teeth mourn in black for the loss on't. This makes your young gallants smell them nine days before they see them, like young pups. This drug is precious and dear. What's this? Oh, this is the spirit of roses: nineteen bushels and a half of roses make but an ounce and a dram on't. 'Tis made of the quintessence of the water after the fifteenth distillation; none may kiss a lady after she hath anointed her lips with this under the degree of a lord at least. 'Tis worth nine pounds an ounce, yet I could never still it so.

Enter [ANTIFRONT] *disguised* [*as an apothecary*]

Antifront Save you, Signor.

Alunio Y'are welcome sir, what do ye lack?

Antifront I want a service and am by my profession an apothecary, and shall be glad to be entertained by you.

Alunio What countryman art thou?

Antifront I am a Florentine born.

Alunio Thou art my countryman and therefore welcome; and in happy time, for I am bound for Italy and want a man to take charge of my shop. Only this is all I shall require of you: be careful of your cares and obedient to your mistress.

Antifront I shall remember still not to forget what you give me in charge.

Alunio What is thy name?

Antifront Giacomo.

Alunio Well, Giacomo, if I find thee honest thou shalt find me liberal.

Antifront I would be loath to be found otherwise.

Alunio Continue so, I prithee, and so farewell, Jaques. But I'll inform my wife before I go to respect thee according to thy merit. *Exit*

Enter PISO *and* [HAVE-LITTLE]

Antifront [*aside*] Now come away my customers; I hope I am fitted for an apothecary. S'heart, I think I'm turned conjurer, for I have no sooner called but the devils are appeared! [*to* PISO *and* HAVE-LITTLE] What do ye lack, gentlemen?

Piso Where's your master, fellow?

Antifront My master is gone into Italy, sir, but if you want anything I'll use you well: if you want any drugs to make lotiums, any restringent powders, any aqua mirabilis, any cordial receipts, or any precious poisons.

Have-Little What poisons have you?

Antifront Excellent good, sir, as ever was tasted. Look you, sir, this poisons by the smell, this by the sight and this by the taste.

Piso Come, give me some of this that poisons by the taste. But how must I use it?

Antifront Put it into a little wine and drink it: 'twill bring you into a long sleep.

Piso But art sure 'twill poison a man?

Antifront Am I sure on't? Why take't upon my credit; 'twill poison any vermin, except it be a woman, for 'twill poison a cat, sir.

Have-Little Why, a cat hath nine lives, sir, and wilt not poison a woman, seeing 'twill poison a cat?

Antifront Oh no! Why, a woman hath nine cats lives; a woman hath more lives than a horse hath diseases, and she will be sometimes in as many minds in an hour as she has lives.

Piso What times are those?

Antifront When she's left a rich merchant's widow, commonly, and hath many suitors. She will in her mind marry three or four and fifty of 'em in an afternoon and threescore more when she goes to bed. Yet in the morning she'll have none of them all, but go to church before day and marry her prentice for the good service 'a did her in her husband's time.

Piso Well. But what's the price of your poison?

Antifront There's an ounce will cost you a French crown, sir.

Have-Little 'Tis very dear.

Antifront Oh, sir, 'tis very cheap, considering the goodness on't.

Piso Yea? Is there good in ill?

Antifront Oh, sir, aye, in many things the better the worser.

Have-Little As how?

Antifront As in poison or in a punk: for the better whore the worser woman ever.

Piso Well, honest fellow, there's thy money and farewell.

Antifront I thank you, sir.

[*Exeunt* PISO *and* HAVE-LITTLE]

I have sold you a poison, my old elders, 'twill make 'em sleep indeed and I thank God that's the worst 'twill do. Well, farewell Master Apothecary; I must now like a friend entreat your shop to have a special care of itself.

Exit

[4.3]

Enter SPARK, RUFFLE *and* PETOUNE

Ruffle And shall we dine with this honourable lord and knight today?

Spark They'll take it unkindly else.

Ruffle Signor, will you go?

Petoune Not I, I was not bid.

Ruffle That's all one, shalt be my guest.

Spark Come, 'a shall go, for there will be his mistress, Madam Fromaga.

Ruffle Nay, then, I know the jet of her complexion will draw the straw of his love thither.

Spark Faith, aye, poor Signor; I see the springle of her

beauty hath already caught the woodcock of his affections.

Petoune Well, I see he that will have the commodity of good wits in his company must endure the discommodity of jests; wit is like the heat of blood in youth, 'twill break out.

Ruffle True, Signor, though it be but on a scab. But come, shall we go?

Petoune Aye, my heroic spirits, I'll follow ye. *Exeunt*

[Act 5, Scene 1]

Enter PETOUNE *one way, and* NAN *the page another way*

Nan Oh, Signor Petoune, what news?

Petoune Faith, ill news. The two Florentine ladies with Master Spark and Master Ruffle were all poisoned yesterday at a feast by your Lord Piso and the knight. But the ladies have recovered their health, but Spark and Ruffle are dead and their burial is committed to Fleer. Your lord and the knight are committed to prison and shall tomorrow be arraigned for the murder and tried by the civil law because your lord is a stranger and claims to be tried by the law of nations.

Nan Faith, Signor, I am very sorry for my lord.

Petoune I protest, sir, so am I for them both.

Nan Well, Signor, I'll commit you to God.

Petoune Let the whole band of angels be sentinels to your safety, sweet sir. *Exeunt*

[5.2]

Enter [ANTIFRONT] *at one door, and* [MITTIMUS] *at another*

Antifront I pray, sir, doth Justice Ferrio dwell here?

Mittimus Yes, sir, 'a dwells here.

Antifront Are you towards him, sir?

Mittimus I am a poor gentleman, whose fortunes much depend upon his favours, and indeed, sir, I am his clerk.

Antifront I pray, sir, your name?

Mittimus My name is Mittimus, sir.

Antifront Good Master Mittimus, I would very willingly speak with your master.

Mittimus Indeed, sir, he's not well, but if you please to send by me the substance of your business, I shall very carefully deliver it.

Antifront Truly, Master Mittimus, my business is but this: tomorrow the Italian lord and Sir John Have-Little are to be arraigned, and your master being the chief judge of the court, without his presence or licence the rest can do nothing. Wherefore Doctor Caius entreats to know his pleasure in this business.

Mittimus Sir, I shall deliver your message and will return his answer to you presently.

Antifront Good Master Mittimus, therein shall you much oblige me to be thankful.

[*Exit* MITTIMUS]

O all-directing power, yield good aspect
And to my purpose give a blessed end.
My intent is good, oh let it so succeed
And be auspicious still to each good deed!

[*Enter* MITTIMUS] *with a ring*

Mittimus Sir, my master hath received your message and hath sent this ring as a token to Doctor Caius, desiring him, since my master's health will not permit him to be present, to proceed alone to judgement. And so commends his love to him.

Antifront Good Master Mittimus, I shall both deliver your master's commendations and the ring.

Exeunt [*in different directions*]

[5.3]

Enter Lord PISO *with a torch, a night-cap, and his doublet open: in prison*

Piso
Still tongueless night put off thy sable robe,
Thou needs not mourn; my villainies were done
By day, thou had'st no hand in them. Oh, I am great
As is a woman that is near her time,
And life's the burthen that I bear!
But 'tis a bastard for that I am asham'd on't.
The law, I hope, is a skilful midwife, and will soon
Deliver me. Grim Justice do thy worst,
Thy cruelty shall prove a courtesy
And bail me out of prison.
Lie there, thou self-consuming taper,
True pattern of my life: I have consum'd
Myself for others, as thou hast done for me,
And now she has extinguished my life,
As I this light. [*puts out the torch*]
Oh, how obedient was my bounty still
To her command! My liberality

Did fatten mischief and hath made her proud.
Oh, that too much of anything should be
So ill in everything!
The sun's all-seeing eye
With too much untemperate heat
Makes wither what it made to flourish;
The earth, being mother to all wholesome herbs,
With too much fatness oft produceth weeds.
A suit of cloth doth keep the body warm
When richer garments makes the wearer proud.
Oh, the mean's the sweetest music;
Contentment revels when that string is touch'd!
But, oh, the time will come she will repent
My death; for when she looks on vice's face
Unmask'd like mine, she will detest and loathe it.
For this is truth and evermore hath been:
None can forsake before he knows his sin. *Exit*

[5.4]

Enter [ANTIFRONT], SPARK, *and* RUFFLE

Antifront Come, come, thou didst but dream thou wert in hell.

Spark I tell thee, I was in hell.

Ruffle And so was I too, I'll be sworn.

Antifront And how long wast e'er thou cam'st thither?

Spark Methought 'twas long, as long as a suit hangs here in the law ere it be ended.

Antifront But, I prithee, how broad was the way to hell?

Spark As broad as the space between two lines in a

chancery bill.

Antifront O sir, there's the conscience on't: say the plaintiff be in one line and the defendant in another, they being enemies, were't either conscience or honesty in the clerk to thrust them so near together that they might go together by th'ears? But, i'faith, what good fellowship was there in hell?

Spark Oh, the devils are excellent companions; they'll out-drink your Dutch captains or court ladies' sponges.

Antifront Who didst see there?

Spark Faith, I saw the four sons of Aymon, and they were porters ever since there was a company made of 'em.

Antifront Why, are there a company of porters in hell?

Spark Oh, aye, the devils are but our apes, man.

Antifront But didst thou see more of them that were damned?

Spark Yes, I saw a citizen damned for refusing a desperate debt because 'twas tendered him on a sabbath.

Antifront I hope we shall have no more citizens damned for that fault.

Spark There was a poor mercenary woman damned because she forsook her trade and turned puritan.

Antifront And good reason! Why could not she have kept her trade and been a puritan, as well as a puritan keep her religion and yet be of her trade?

Spark There was a lady damned because she never painted, a puritan for saying grace without turning up the white of his eyes, a tailor for never having scabby fingers, a vintner for making great two pennyworths of sugar. But there was an Inns of Court man damned, and I was sorry for him.

Antifront Why was he damned?

Spark Alas, for a small fault.

Antifront I prithee, what wast?

Spark For having always money in his purse.

Antifront Were there no lawyers in hell?

Spark There were none of your great lawyers, as your sergeants and benchers, for they take council of too many good angels to come there. But your young puny lawyers, they were in swarms like gnats in summer.

Antifront Why, are there so many of them there?

Spark Alas, man, they seldom converse with a good angel – scarce once in a whole Michaelmas Term – and if 'a come, 'a stays not long with 'em to feed these souls, for they are fain to send 'em away straight to pay for the feeding of their horses. There was a chambermaid damned for keeping her virginity till she was married, and there were many soldiers damned for saying their prayers when they were drunk.

Antifront [*to* RUFFLE] But what didst thou see in hell?

Ruffle Oh, I saw a scrivener damned for procuring a gentleman money *gratis*, but I came in an excellent time.

Antifront What time wast?

Ruffle In a gossiping time, for Proserpina was newly brought a-bed of two twins.

Antifront Two twins! What were they?

Ruffle A sergeant and a yeoman, but she has put them out to nurse.

Antifront I prithee, where?

Ruffle Faith, at the counter in Wood Street, and the slaves will suck already like little horseleeches.

Antifront But when will she have 'em home, that we may be rid of 'em?

Ruffle Faith, she's an unnatural mother, she cares not greatly if they never come home. But the devil their father he loves 'em well, he'll have 'em home again e'er long.

Antifront Which is the elder brother?

Ruffle Oh, the sergeant: the devil allows him the better maintenance, for he has more to the dressing of his meat.

Antifront Well, gentlemen, since by the heavens' pleasure I have been appointed to save your lives, let me entreat you to keep yourselves secret till the sequel of this action shall need your presence.

Ruffle Come, let's go, we'll only follow your directions.

Exeunt

[5.5]

Enter [*Doctor* CAIUS *and* SECOND JUDGE] *with their train, and sit down*

First Jailor Will't please ye have the prisoners brought forth?

Caius We can do nothing till we hear from Doctor Ferrio, to know his pleasure in these proceedings.

Second Judge Was any man sent to him?

Caius Yes, Fleer, the Lady Florida's man, which is not yet returned.

Enter [SECOND JAILOR]

Second Jailor Reverend judges, here's a doctor at door desires admittance.

Caius Entreat him to come in.

Enter [ANTIFRONT] *like a doctor*

Antifront Learned doctors, Doctor Ferrio commends him to you, and, because sickness hath laid so strong a hand upon his weak decrepit body, which doth detain his presence, he entreats you to accept of me in his place. And as assurance of his earnest desire thereof he has sent this well-known ring as a token to you.

Caius Sir, we know the ring and you are very welcome. And so, I pray 'e, assume his place.

First Jailor [*to* CAIUS] Is it your pleasure the prisoners be brought forth?

Caius Aye, both of them.

Enter PISO, [HAVE-LITTLE], [FLORIDA *and* FELECIA], NAN *and* SU[SAN], PETOUNE, [*and*] FROMAGA

Caius [*to* PISO] My lord, you are here indicted of a hateful crime, and I am very sorry to see you in this sort stand here.

Piso Thrice reverend judges and therefore honoured lords, I must confess that like a skilful dancer I have truly footed folly, yet, like a learner in my course of life trod much out of measure, I have lived like an unbacked colt, proud and wanton. My tree of life hath born more leaves than fruit; I ever was debauched and steered away my days even in a sea of sin.

Caius And in that sea, my lord, you bore so great a sail as you have overset your barque of life. And here you are accused, my lord, even of a hateful crime – so is the knight there – for poisoning two gentlemen, Spark and Ruffle. How do you answer this, my lord?

Piso Alas, my lord, this is soon answered, for though that I have surfeited on sin yet have I not been drunk with blood.

Caius [*to* HAVE-LITTLE] What say you, knight?

Have-Little The crime is great, I must confess, my lord, but I am sure the proof can be but little.

Caius [*to* FELECIA *and* FLORIDA] Ladies, you know most and therefore 'tis fittest most you speak.

Florida Why then, my lord, this is all we can say: this lord and knight feasted divers of us their friends, but four of us he drenched with such a dram, which soon made two discharge the debt they owed to nature.

Piso [*aside*] O conscience, would'st thou give me leave!

Felecia And we no doubt, my lords, had long e'er this breathed out our lives, like them, but that we had the lesser quantity; for being esteemed the weaker vessels they thought the lesser blow would break us.

Have-Little [*aside*] Oh, had not death arrested me!

Antifront Why then, my lord, we thus must now proceed: they that spilt innocent blood themselves must bleed. But, ladies, I have heard you had a man called Fleer, what's become of him?

Florida He was sent to Doctor Ferrio and we never saw him since.

Antifront Do you know his hand, ladies?

Felecia Very well.

Antifront I pray look here then.

Florida This is his hand indeed.

Felecia I very perfectly do know it to be his.

Antifront Why, then, upon this hand I here arrest you both upon your lives.

Both Who, we?

Antifront Aye, you, ladies. [*to* CAIUS] My lord, I pray you read this letter.

Caius [*Reads*] 'Reverend judges, God will by some means punish every sin and though against my will, yet by my conscience I am enforced to unmask my ladies' villainies. The murder for which the lord and knight are like to die was first plotted by them: the two pages with myself did hear it. The prisoners in this action are enforced by sacrament to be secret. And, thus entreating heaven in justice still to aid you, yours, Fleer, a Florentine.' [*to* PISO] Is this true, my lord?

Second Judge They are sworn not to reveal it.

Antifront But being revealed, they may affirm it.

Both 'Tis too true, my lord.

Antifront Where are the pages?

[NAN *and* SUSAN *come forward*]

Both Here, my lord.

Antifront How say you, boys, to this letter?

Both The letter speaks nothing but the truth.

Antifront Well, ladies, then we here pronounce this sentence: that you must die among the rest.

Florida You powers divine, I now do plainly see
Heaven's starry eyes sees all our villainy,
And God in justice murder will reveal.
[*to* PISO] But were I now my life for to begin
I'd be an honest wife to you.

Wherefore forgive me, dearest lord.

Piso Lady, I do, even as I hope to be forgiven.

Felecia Show mercy, heaven, my sins do thee offend;
There's none can say he's happy till his end.
[*to* HAVE-LITTLE]
Forgiveness, knight, and since the law on us
Hath laid so strict a hand, oh let me be
Thy wife before I die, and were I now
A thousand years to live I would be honest,
Loving none but thee.

Have-Little I do forgive you, lady, with my soul.

Enter a MESSENGER *with letters to* PISO

Messenger Long live my honoured lord and mighty Duke of Florence.

Piso So 'a will, as long as't please the hangman.

Messenger My honoured lord, your father is deceased and the state of Florence by me hath sent their letters and allegiance.

Piso Let them call back the banished Signor Antifront, whom they, and we and all have wronged. Oh, could I live but to inquire him out, in satisfaction of his wrongs I'd marry his eldest daughter and whilst 'a lived 'a should be restored to his estate! But oh, he's –

Fleer shows himself to be ANTIFRONT

Antifront Here, my lord.
I tax you to your word; Signor Antifront yet lives.
And here's his elder daughter, whom himself

But now condemn'd to die. [*to* HAVE-LITTLE]
And here's the younger left for you.

[*Enter* SPARK *and* RUFFLE]

The poisoned men are here alive again,
Who did but dream of death,
[*to* NAN *and* SUSAN]
but yet do
Live t'enrich a nuptial bed to you two.
And now, since ev'rything so well doth sort,
Let all be pleased in this our comic sport.
Where's Petoune? He shall have his mistress too:
He most deserves, for he did hotly woo.
[*to audience*] If we part friends your hands unto
us lend,
What was not well we'll next strive to amend.
Exeunt omnes

FINIS

Glossarial Notes

All references to Shakespeare are to *The Arden Shakespeare Complete Works*, ed. Richard Proudfoot, Ann Thompson and David Scott Kastan (Walton-on-Thames: Thomas Nelson, 1998). All references to works in the 'Beaumont and Fletcher' canon are to Fredson Bowers, gen. ed., *The Dramatic Works in the Beaumont and Fletcher Canon*, 10 vols (Cambridge: Cambridge University Press, 1968-1996). All references to the plays of Dekker (with the exception of *Blurt Master Constable*) are to Fredson Bowers, ed., *The Dramatic Works of Thomas Dekker* (Cambridge: Cambridge University Press, 1953-1961). Other dramatic texts are cited from modern editions; where none are available early texts have been used (these are cited by signature number rather than page number). I have regularised 'u' and 'v' and 'i' and 'j'; spelling is otherwise unamended. For these early texts, dates of performance are given before dates of original publication: e.g. '(*c.* 1615; London, 1616)'. References for other frequently-cited sources are as follows:

Leggatt – Alexander Leggatt, 'The Plays of Edward Sharpham: An Introduction and a Commentary', unpublished MA thesis, University of Birmingham, 1963

Linthicum – Marie C. Linthicum, *Costume in the Drama of Shakespeare and his Contemporaries* (Oxford: Clarendon Press, 1936)

Nibbe – Hunold Nibbe, ed., *The Fleire*, Materialien zur Kunde des älteren englischen Dramas (London: David Nott, 1912)

OED – *Oxford English Dictionary*, second edition (1989)

Petter – Christopher Gordon Petter, *A Critical Old Spelling Edition of the Works of Edward Sharpham* (New York: Garland, 1986)

Pollard – Tanya Pollard, 'The Pleasures and Perils of Smoking in Early Modern England', in *Smoke: A Global History of Smoking*, ed. Sander Gilman and Zhou Xun (London: Reaktion Books, 2004), 38-45

Sugden – E.H. Sugden, *A Topographical Dictionary to the Works of Shakespeare and his Fellow Dramatists* (Manchester: Manchester University Press, 1925)

Tilley – M.P. Tilley, *A Dictionary of the Proverbs in England in the Sixteenth and Seventeenth Centuries* (Ann Arbor: University of Michigan Press, 1950)

Williams – Gordon Williams, *A Dictionary of Sexual Language and Imagery in Shakespearean and Stuart Literature* (London: Athlone, 1994)

To the Reader and Hearer

1 *perusers* readers

4 *laugh, and lie down* proverbial (Tilley, L92), often with sexual connotations; cf. Dekker, *News from Graves-end* (London, 1604): 'As for the women, they may laugh and lye downe, its a merry world with them but some-body pays for it' (sig. B4r)

7 *forfeits* penalties for breach of contract

10 *viz.* that is to say (abbreviation of *videlicet*)

i'th' in the

i'th' country during periods of plague, Londoners often took refuge in the countryside (where they were not always welcome). *Country* often invokes a sexual pun; cf. Shakespeare, *Hamlet* (*c.* 1600): 'Do you think I meant country matters?' (3.2.118)

12 *apological* apologetic or in justification

13 *his first Minerva* his first brainchild or literary production; Minerva was legendarily born out of the head of Jove. This might not be strictly true, if Petter is right in attributing the prose pamphlet *The Discovery of the Knights of the Post* (1597) to Sharpham.

19-20 *you … affections* Sharpham's *Cupid's Whirligig*, written for the Children of the King's Revels, was entered in the Stationers' Register by John Busby and Arthur Johnson on 26 June 1607 and printed in the same year by Edward Allde for Arthur Johnson. Allde also printed *The Fleer* for Francis Burton.

21 *through … field* sounds proverbial but is not recorded by Tilley

22 *modicum* a small quantity

Dramatis Personae

The early editions have no *dramatis personae*; this list has been compiled with reference to those provided by Petter and Leggatt

2 *ANTIFRONT* Italian: 'contrary face'. In *A World of Words* (London, 1598), John Florio translates *anti* as 'a word much used in composition before other words, signifying contrarietie to or against' (sig. B5r) and *fronte* as 'a front, a forhead, a brow, the space or forfront of a squadron or battell' (sig. M4v). Antifront's name also relates to the disguised duke Altofronto ('lofty-brow') in Marston's *The Malcontent* (*c.* 1603) and the 'converted courtesan' Bellafront ('beautiful face') in Dekker and Middleton's *The Honest Whore* (*c.* 1605).

3 *Fleer* *to fleer* means to mock or jeer: the name Fleer embodies the nature of Antifront's alter-ego. It also refers to Marston's *The Fawn*, where the disguised duke Hercules takes on the persona of a flattering and servile

courtier called Fawn.

4 *FLORIDA* flowering; flowery

5 *FELECIA* happy (from Latin *felix*); now more commonly spelled Felicia

6 *FROMAGA* the lady-in-waiting's name probably involves a bawdy pun: Williams (1: 232) notes that cheese is often used allusively to refer to women. Cf. *The First Part of Jeronimo* (*c*. 1602), in *Thomas Kyd, The Spanish Tragedy with Anonymous: The First Part of Jeronimo*, ed. Emma Smith (London: Penguin, 1998): 'thers a morrall in that, as much / To say knavery in the Court and honesty in a / Cheese house' (6.86-8); Heywood, *The Iron Age* (*c*. 1613; London, 1631): 'by this hee's gnawing *Menelaus* Cheese' (sig. D3v).

12 *SPARK* carries connotations of brightness and liveliness, but also refers to elegant or foppish young men or to those who try to be smart in their manner or clothing (*OED* spark *n.*^{2} 2)

13 *RUFFLE* as well as the reference to clothing, *OED* notes that 'to ruffle' can mean 'to handle (a woman) with rude familiarity', a usage it dates to 1607 (ruffle *v.*^{2} 4b)

15 *PISO* Leggatt suggests that Sharpham here recalls Marston's *What You Will* (*c*. 1601), ed. M.R. Woodhead (Nottingham: Nottingham University Press, 1980): 'The sprightful Piso, the great Florentine' (1.1.353)

16 *PETOUNE* a variant spelling of *petun*, a native South American word for tobacco adopted by the English (*OED*, Leggatt)

19 *MITTIMUS* a warrant directed to the keeper of a prison, ordering him to receive into custody and hold in safe-keeping the person sent and specified in the warrant; colloquially, to get your mittimus could mean to get the sack (*OED*)

1.1

15 *puissant* powerful

20 *Phaeton in pride did ride* Phaeton was the son of Helios (the sun) in classical mythology, who died when he borrowed his father's chariot and lost control of it; used allusively to refer to foolish or reckless behaviour

22 *your celsitude* your highness

26-7 *disguisement ... laws* taking on this disguise would be too extreme a measure if the heavens were smiling on me, but (because they are not) I am ruled by them

29 *cuor forte rompe cativa sorte* a stout heart breaks down evil fortune (H.P. Jones, ed., *Dictionary of Foreign Phrases and Classical Quotations* [Edinburgh: J. Grant, 1923], p. 414)

1.2

0.1-4 *Enter ... SERVING-MEN* the massed entrance is perhaps intended to give the audience the impression that Florida and Felecia have retained their status as the daughters of a duke, an impression which is rudely shattered by the ensuing dialogue

3 *base* morally suspect, despicable; of low social status

4 *place* rank, status

8-9 *'t had* it had ('it would have been')

12 *the letter law* the letter of the law

14 *of two ... chosen* proverbial (Tilley, E207: 'Of two Evils (ills) choose the least')

15-16 *But had we* but even if we had another way of making a living

16 *art* artifice, deceit (i.e. cosmetics)

19 *want* greed

23 *curbed* restrained

28 *state* manner or way of existing

29 *strangers* foreigners

31 *friends* lovers

33 *fashion* (1) clothing; (2) behaviour
Florence the city of Florence is the former home of Florida and Felecia, but Sharpham perhaps plays on his audience's knowledge that this was also an archetypal name for a prostitute; in *The Honest Lawyer* (*c.* 1615; London, 1616) a women pretending to a prostitute calls herself Florence, and the bawd comments, 'I like the name well. Its a lucky name to make a whore on' (sig. B1r) (Williams, 1: 516-17)

1.3

5 *'A* he (see Textual Notes introduction)
8 *forsooth* truly
11-12 *gentleman usher* originally a gentleman whose duty was to walk in front of a person of high rank. Later indicates a male servant who attends a lady and sometimes provides sexual 'service' to her (Williams, 2: 593).
15 *By my troth* a mild expletive (*troth*: truth)
23 *inward* (sexually) intimate
25 *secrets* sexual organs (*OED* secret *a.* and *n.* 6. *pl.*)
26 *tables* writing tablet
28 *Pluck out your pin* (1) get out your pen[cil] (2) get out your penis (Williams, 2: 1032-4). Fromaga's speeches are a series of relentless *double entendres*.
29 *standing bare* bareheaded (i.e. without a hat), but with sexual implication (*to stand*: to have an erection [*OED* stand *v.* 6c])
33-4 *half a crown* English coin worth 2 shillings and 6 pence, in circulation from the late fifteenth century
39 *band* collar or ruff (Linthicum, pp. 155-7)
40 *shirt* garment with a high neck and long sleeves, worn as an undergarment and as night clothes (Linthicum, pp. 213, 215). Often used as the male counterpart of the woman's smock in innuendo (Williams, 3: 1235).

43 *periwig* wig; may also allude to the chronic hair-loss which was a symptom of syphilis (Williams, 2: 639-41)

44-5 *hatched sword* engraved or inlaid with ornamentation; *sword* can also refer to the penis and the Gentleman's next line picks up this *double entendre*

46 *his* Sir John Have-Little's

47 *service* (1) employment; (2) sexual action

48-9 *wear it by your office* wear it by virtue of your office

49 *is your cloak lined through?* servants were generally supposed not to wear cloaks, and to have a cloak lined through was expensive and therefore a mark of rank (Linthicum, pp. 193-5). The exchange and the lines that follow also quibble on *line*: copulate; cf. Shakespeare, *As You Like It* (*c.* 1600): 'Winter'd garments must be lin'd, / So must slender Rosalind' (3.2.102-3) (Williams, 2: 816-17)

50 *good depth* (1) lined some of the way in; (2) refers to sexual penetration

51-2 *Your ladies … credit* (1) having their servants well-dressed will reflect well on Florida and Felecia; (2) as prostitutes they make money from sexual activity

52 *credit* (1) profit; (2) honour, reputation

53 *hangers* (1) straps on a belt from which the scabbard of a sword was hung: 'Hangers, especially wrought or embroidered, were gifts of ladies to their favourites' (Linthicum, p. 265); (2) testicles

54-5 *a pair of mine own* picks up Fromaga's *double entendre* in the previous line and again equates hangers and testicles

56 *in trouble* (1) at the pawnbroker's; (2) diseased

58-9 *you … service* (1) you have been unemployed; (2) you have gone a long time without sex

61 *By'r Lady* By our Lady: a mild expletive (*Lady*: the Virgin Mary)

63 *busy* engaging in sexual activity

69 *up and bare* (1) bare-headed; (2) naked

71 *stand … head* with a sexual pun on having an erection

72 *place* situation, job

79 *makes tender* presents for approval, offers (*OED* tender *v.*[1] 2)

81 *Kiss your hand* 'the current fashion of the high ranking and of women was to greet by kissing their own hands' (Petter); Antifront's comment at 2.1.248-9 might suggest that by the early seventeenth century it was considered characteristic of servants, but Have-Little is also reported to have kissed his hand to Nan and Susan (2.1.404-5)

83 *beholding* obliged (*OED* beholding *ppl. a.* 1)

85 *parts* (1) characteristics, attributes (*OED* part *n.* 12); (2) genitals

89 *begotten* conceived

inn's court (1) courtyard of an inn; (2) Inn of Court (one of four centres for legal training in London)

90-1 *he … house* membership of the Inns of Court was thought to confer gentility on a student, whatever his social background

99 *in common* used or enjoyed by a number of persons (*OED* common *n.* 13d)

and must and you must; the personal pronoun is omitted to give an impression of colloquial conversation (see Charles Barber, *Early Modern English*, second edition [Edinburgh: Edinburgh University Press, 1997], pp. 200-1)

101 *t'other* the other

107 *tongues* (1) (foreign) languages; (2) sexual prowess; (3) alludes to oral sex. Compare Shakespeare, *Cymbeline* (*c.* 1610-11): 'if you can penetrate her with your fingering, so: we'll try with tongue too' (2.3.14-15); see Williams, 3: 1401-2.

112 *a wild speech* Irish Gaelic was perceived by the English

to be an uncivilised language; cf. Shakespeare, *1 Henry IV* (*c.* 1596), where Hotspur declares that he 'had rather hear Lady, my brach, howl in Irish' than listen to Mortimer's daughter sing in Welsh (3.1.230). Also alludes to the English tendency to refer to the native Irish as 'the Wild Irish', in contrast to the Protestant settlers of the Pale; cf. Webster, *The White Devil* (1612), ed. Christina Luckyj (London: A&C Black, 1996): 'Like the wild Irish I'll ne'er count thee dead / Till I can play at football with thy head' (4.1.136-7) (Sugden).

114 *Has travelled* (He) has travelled: see note to l. 99

118-19 *your ladyship … than he* Felecia is (a) more sexually experienced, or (b) more likely to suffer from venereal disease than the Gentleman. Fromaga makes a conventional association between France and syphilis (known as the French disease or French pox) and between France and promiscuous behaviour (Williams; Sugden). Compare Dekker and Webster, *Westward Ho* (*c.* 1604), where Justiniano tells the bawd Birdlime 'you may speake French; most of your kinds can understand French' (1.1.127-8)

123 *pray 'e* pray ye (see Textual Notes introduction)

125 *bare standing* inadequate and fixed (*OED* bare *adj.* 10b; standing *ppl. a.* 14a); with sexual pun (cf. 1.3.29, 71, 99)

126 *forty shillings a year* *shilling*: coin worth twelve pence or one twentieth of a pound. Forty shillings (or £2) per year would be a low wage for a high-status servant; Fleer pitties the 'poor slave' who has 'but seven shillings a week board wages' (2.1.11-12).

128 *countenance* patronage (*OED* countenance *n.* 8)

130 *'t 'as* it has

131 *court-maintenance* living at court

132 *countenance* face (*OED* countenance *n.* 5)

135 *silly* harmless, unsophisticated

137 *bounty* generosity

140 *brave* fine, splendid

141 *serve* (1) assist; (2) provide sexual service

abroad out of doors

1.4

2 *stand* picks up the pun from 1.3

8 *last day* yesterday

10-12 *Oh … thine* paraphrases Leander's courtship of Hero in Marlowe's *Hero and Leander* (1592): 'I would my rude words had the influence / To lead thy thoughts, as thy fair looks do mine, / Then shouldst thou be his prisoner who is thine' (*Hero and Leander*, in *Christopher Marlowe: The Complete Poems and Translations*, ed. Stephen Orgel (Harmondsworth: Penguin, 1971), 1.200-2). Cf. Jonson, *Every Man in his Humour* (1598), ed. Robert Miola (Manchester: Manchester University Press, 2000), in which Matheo tries to pass these lines off as his own (3.4.62-4). Elizabethan erotic poetry is frequently quoted by tongue-tied suitors in early seventeenth century plays; cf. *The Fair Maid of the Exchange* (*c.* 1602; London, 1607), in which Bowdler's misappropriation of lines from Shakespeare's *Venus and Adonis* is met with derision by Mall Berry.

14 *Hellespont* the sea separating the lovers in *Hero and Leander*, in which they eventually drown

16-17 *Oh … rough* paraphrases the next lines of Leander's speech in *Hero and Leander*: 'Be not unkind and fair; misshapen stuff / Are of behaviour boisterous and rough' (1.203-4)

20-23 *he was … stubble* Nibbe and Petter compare Shakespeare, *1 Henry IV*: 'Came there a certain lord, neat and trimly dress'd, / Fresh as a bridegroom, and his chin new reap'd / Show'd like a stubble-land at harvest-home.'

(1.3.32-4)

22 *marry* a mild expletive (corruption of 'Mary')

25 *living* income

28 *sweat* (1) a sign of sexual exertion; (2) a symptom of and treatment for syphilis (Williams, 3: 1343-4)

29-30 *Man was made to labour … women to bear* (1) A man's role in life is to work … a woman's role is to have children; (2) A man's role in life is to exert himself sexually … a woman's role is to lie back and endure it

29 *to labour* (1) to perform manual work; (2) to exert oneself sexually (Williams, 2: 773-4)

30 *creation* the purpose for which I was created

bear (1) to give birth to children (*OED* bear *v.*[1] 43); (2) to have sex. Compare Middleton, *Michaelmas Term* (*c.* 1605), in *A Mad World My Masters and Other Plays*, ed. Michael Taylor (Oxford: Oxford University Press, 1995): 'they're ordained to sweat for gentlemen; porters' backs and women's bellies bear up the world' (2.3.313-14) (Williams, 1: 85-6).

31 *birds to fly, fish to swim* see Genesis 1:28 ('And God blessed them, and God said to them Bring foorth fruite and multiply, and fill the earth, and subdue it, and rule over the fish of the sea, and over the foule of the heavens, and over every beast that mooveth upon the earth'); Psalms 8: 6-8

34 *punk* prostitute (*OED* punk *n.*[1])

to do (1) to attend to, to be associated with (*OED* do *v.* 11a); (2) to have sexual intercourse with (late usage recorded in *OED* do *v.* 16b)

35-7 *his wit … wit* he has as little money as he has wit, and vice versa

40 *conditions* character, morals (*OED* condition *n.* 10a, 11b. *pl.*)

44 *sympathize* represent by something corresponding or

fitting (*OED* sympathize *v.* 3)

49 *felicity* intense happiness

59 *God't* God it

67 *Ruffle* Although the quarto has the speech-prefix '*Ruff.*' it is possible that Have-Little originally spoke this line. Such a reading gives greater symmetry on stage, and it was adopted in the Globe Education staged reading of *The Fleer* in June 2004.

69 *caper* dance merrily, skip (*OED* caper *v.*[1])

71-2 *a sober measure* a slow dance or slow tempo (*OED* has 'grave or stately': measure *n.* 19, 20a)

73-4 *Ladies … here* sentence structure is more fluid in early modern English; *here* can refer either to the whole sentence ('we have come here to introduce you to a gentleman') or to the noun phrase ('we have come to introduce you to this gentleman')

77-8 *traveller and a great tobacconist* tobacco was still an exotic commodity, and it is implied that Petoune has taken up smoking on his travels. In *Work for Chimney-Sweepers, or, A Warning for Tobacconists* (London, 1601), Joseph Hall criticises 'our smoky gallants, who having long time glutted themselves with the fond fopperies and fashions of our neighbour Countries: yet still desirous of novelties, have not stucke to travell as farre as *India* to fetch a *Dulce venenum* [sweet poison], a graecian *Helen*, an insatiate *Messaline*, and hugge a stinging serpent in their bosomes' (sig. A.iii.r) (Pollard)

78 *tobacconist* user of tobacco. The play capitalises on the varied associations of tobacco, seen as an unhygienic nuisance, an exotic and un-English habit, an anaphrodisiac and as having a feminising or enervating influence. It is also seen as a possible cure for syphilis, owing to the theory that cures for diseases could be found in the places where the disease originated (syphilis

was sometimes thought to have come from the New World). In 'A Counterblast to Tobacco' (1604), King James draws a direct correlation between the introduction of tobacco and syphilis into Britain from the New World: 'as from them was first brought into Christendome, that most detestable disease; so from them likewise was brought this use of *Tobacco*' (*Works* [London, 1616], p. 214) (Pollard). See also the punchline to Sir John Davies' Epigram 36, 'Of Tobacco' (1590), in *The Poems of Sir John Davies*, ed. Robert Krueger (Oxford: Clarendon Press, 1975): 'it the pox wil cure: / This were inough, without discoursing more, / All our brave gallants in the town t'alure' (p. 144).

80 *purification* cleansing, especially after child-birth

83 *moon-calf* fool; also means a false conception or a monstrous birth, so links with l. 79

84-90 *Faith … toys* in Petoune's hyperbolic conviction that tobacco is an effective cure-all, Sharpham satirizes early Jacobean pro-tobacco rhetoric

86 *mundify* cleanse or purify

95-6 *wisdom … him* draws on Proverbs 1: 20 ('Wisedome crieth without: she uttereth her voice in the streetes') – 1: 24 ('Because I have called, and ye refused: I have stretched out mine hand, and none would regard'); see also Shakespeare, *1 Henry IV*: 'wisdom cries out in the streets and no man regards it' (1.2.87-8)

98 *arrantest* most good for nothing

woodcock fool: woodcocks were notoriously easy to catch

103 *puppy* a vain and foolish young man

104 *very* genuine, complete

105 *egregious* remarkable

106 *coxcomb* a fool or simpleton, can also mean a fop

116 *complexion of thy nose* red noses often indicate self-

indulgent behaviour, either drinking or smoking; cf. Shakespeare's Bardolph in *1 Henry IV*: 'thou art our admiral, thou bearest the lantern in the poop, but 'tis in the nose of thee: thou art the Knight of the Burning Lamp' (3.3.25-7) (Nibbe, Petter). The nose is also key to jokes about venereal disease, since its disintegration was a symptom of syphilis. As noted above, tobacco and syphilis were closely associated in this period.

119 *take anything in snuff* take offence at anything. According to *OED*, the practice of taking snuff (powered tobacco which is sniffed through the nose) did not become fashionable in England until around 1680, though it seems to have been popular in Ireland and Scotland at an earlier date. There are, however, earlier references to tobacco being sniffed: Samuel Rowlands in 'The Devil's Health-Drinker' argues that 'A meale a day's inough, / Take out Tobacco for the rest, / By pipe or else by snuffe' and notes that tobacco 'worketh sundry waies', 'The leafe greene, drie, steept, burnd, the dust / Have each their speciall praise'. *The Knave of Clubs* (London, 1609), sig. F1v.

131 *Dear* (1) beloved; (2) expensive

135 *apothecary* tradesman who prepares and sells drugs for medicinal purposes

140 *yond'* yonder

147 *Every fool can say aye and no* may be proverbial, but it is not recorded by Tilley

153-4 *this … foot* signifies Petoune's willingness to court either Nan or Susan, drawing on the proverbs 'He that serves everybody is paid by nobody' and 'A common man is no man's servant' (Tilley, S244, S231).

153-4 *upright shoe* (1) a type of shoe that can be worn on either foot; (2) an erect penis (*upright*: having an erection; *shoe*: male genitals)

154 *serve either foot* *serve* has the now-familiar sexual pun and *foot* in this case refers to the female genitals (Williams, 1: 524-5)

156 *mettle* (1) constitution, character; (2) metal

162-3 *Copper ... is* (1) red in colour (see note to l. 116); (2) alludes to the metal nose worn by someone whose nose has been eaten away by syphilis. Cf. Marston, *Antonio's Revenge* (c. 1600), ed. Reavley Gair (Manchester: Manchester University Press, 1978): 'Truth is the touchstone of all things and if your nose will not abide the truth, your nose will not abide the touch; and if your nose will not abide the touch, your nose is a copper nose and must be nailed up for a slip' (1.3.16-20), a slip being a counterfeit coin. Cf. also Jonson, *Bartholomew Fair* (1614), ed. G.R. Hibbard (London: Ernest Benn, 1977): 'the hole in the nose here of some tobacco-takers' (2.6.44).

167 *cold comfort* poor or inadequate consolation. Proverbial (Tilley, C542).

175 *blind-man's-buff* game in which one player is blindfolded and has to catch and identify the others. Also used as euphemism for copulation, cf. John Day, *Humour out of Breath* (1607-8; London, 1608): 'One that I stumbled on at Blindman buffe; a proper man, a man every inch of him' (H2v); Middleton, *A Mad World My Masters* (c. 1605), in *A Mad World My Masters and Other Plays*, ed. Taylor: 'Cupid plays best at blindman buff' (3.3.97).

176 *bobbed* (1) cheated, made a fool of or mocked (*OED* bob *v.*[1] 1-2); (2) hit (*OED* bob *v.*[2] 1); (3) had a sexual encounter (Williams, 1: 123-4); (4) alludes to various games called 'bob-fool', 'bob-her', 'bob and hit' etc. (*OED* bob *v.*[1] 3)

177 *Prithee* (I) pray thee

177-8 *Dear lady … tobacco* sharing a pipe was a sign of male friendship; cf. William Barclay, *Nepenthes, or The Virtues of Tobacco* (London, 1614), who writes that tobacco 'worketh never so well, as when it is given from man to man, as a pledge of friendshippe and amitie' (sig. A4r) (Pollard). Petoune's offering a pipe to a woman is perhaps, therefore, socially aberrant even before it is found to be empty.

181 *empty pipe* the empty tobacco pipe alludes to Petoune's sexual failure (Williams, 2: 1040, 3: 1399-1400), an association which the following lines make even clearer

185 *how now* what's the meaning of this?

186 *fitter … on* alludes to the sharpening of knifes on a block (*whet*: sharpen)

190 *Indian plant* tobacco, referring to its original location – the 'Occidental Indias' of the New World (Pollard)

197 *have no face to speak* have no pretext to speak; cannot put a good construction on (*OED* face *n.* 10a)

198 *element* preferred surroundings

201-2 *ask … knees* kneeling is 'allusive of sexual posture' (Williams, 2: 764). Petoune's apology is staged as a quasi-sexual performance which, like his offering an empty pipe, suggests his sexual incompetence.

210 *on's* on his

214-5 *hath … snuff* has made you justifiably angry

227-8 *he … stoop* he must abase/humiliate himself, playing on *stoop*, which is allusive of sexual compliance (see Williams, s.v. *bend*)

230 *minister't* minister it; pronounce it

243 *repeating* telling other people about

244 *censing* perfumed with odours from burning incense
unguents ointments or salves

248 *squibs and smoke squirts* flashes of fire (*squib*: firework) and smoke coming from Petoune's pipe, with a pun on

squirt: (1) orgasm and (2) a syringe for the treatment of syphilis (see Williams, 3: 1299-1300). Petoune is not to bother the women with either his tobacco or his unwanted sexual advances.

263 *comb for any case* *case*: (1) sexual organ, and (2) (less often) brothel (see Williams, 1: 211-13); *comb* probably means coxcomb. The phrase may mean that Petoune (1) is willing to court any woman, or (2) will have to resort to paying for sex in future.

267 *God be w'ye* God be with you

268 *some shall smoke for this* (1) be angry about this; (2) suffer as a result of this (*OED* smoke *v*. 3-4)

272 *slight* (1) smooth or sleek; (2) slender; (3) flimsy (*OED* slight *adj*. 1-3)

274 *Hey-day* exclamation indicating surprise or happiness

275 *term* period when the law courts held sessions (known as Michaelmas, Hilary, Easter and Trinity terms)

275-6 *thrunged* pushed

277 *I am sick* this line may have had greater impact in the first decade of the seventeenth century, during which plague was endemic in London

292 *then … glasses* (1) reference to the skill of the Italians (Venetians in particular) at making glass (Petter, Leggatt); (2) glass is often used as an 'emblem of a woman's fragile reputation' (Williams, 2: 600); compare the proverbial phrase 'Credit lost is like a Venice glass broke' (Tilley, C814, dated 1614). This sense seems to be picked up by Antifront/Fleer in his reply. That it follows Antifront/Fleer's statement that he is an Italian is appropriate; cf. Middleton and Rowley, *The Spanish Gypsy* (1623; London, 1653), on the rarity of finding 'a Spaniard a drunkard, as a Germane sober, an Italian no Whoremonger, an English man to pay his debts' (sig. B1r)

293 *asses* (1) fools; (2) cuckolds (Williams, 1: 45-6); this image is used in *Knights of the Post* to describe a man who is his own pander: 'the proud foole got on his hollyday cap upon a working day: whereby every boy perceived his asses eares' (Petter, p. 155)

296 *wonnot* would not

298 *walking spur* (1) spur worn for display only; (2) impotent man: Williams notes that spurs are 'symbolic of sexual riding' (3: 1295)

299 *jingles much* makes a lot of noise

he'll never prick (1) such spurs were often unsharpened; (2) never penetrate sexually

304 *pissing while* very short period of time

314 *towards* in attendance on

321 *service* see note to 1.3.47

322 *prefer* (1) put forward, advance; (2) like better (*OED* prefer 1a, 7)

324 *Nay't* Nay, it

327 *served* gave sexual favours to

329 *Y'are* you are

331-2 *You … Italians* reference to the stereotypical Machiavellian Italian of the early modern English stage

332-3 *but … you?* Fleer argues that the English as just as good as killing men as the Italians, but instead of poisoning them, they allow their women to exhaust them sexually

333 *God's light!* a mild expletive

serve (1) be employed by; (2) sexually service

334 *quoth* said

337 *when't* when it

345 *in't* in it

349 *apparel* clothing

2.1

2 *that* that which

8 *ere* before

11-12 *board wages* wages intended to be spent on food

13 *extraordinary* (1) exceptional; (2) additional; (3) not at the ordinary, a kind of tavern where food was served

flesh (1) meat (therefore food); (2) sexual partner

14 *fast* go without food (also implies repentance)

hot lusty

16 *bridle* restrain

17 *surgeon* barber-surgeon, who treats venereal disease

19 *mercenary women* working only for a reward (usually monetary), therefore prostitutes

members parts of society, with a pun on sexual organs (perhaps an implication of unnaturalness, as this term is more often used of the male sexual organs)

21 *familiar* (sexually) intimate

22 *men* servants

24 *penance* discipline or observance, imposed by a priest upon a penitent after confession (*OED* penance *n.* 2)

pains (1) punishment, penalty (*OED* pain *n.* 1 a); (2) physical pain caused by venereal disease

30 *gratis* for free

31 *hugger-mugger* in secret, sometimes with a sexual twist; cf. *Hamlet*: 'we have done but greenly / In hugger-mugger to inter him' (4.5.83-4)

32 *citizen's wife … prentice* apprentices usually lived as part of their master's family, and there are innumerable stories/jokes about illicit relationships between wife and apprentice

33 *practise* work, pursue a career (*OED* practise *v.* 3)

overseer supervisor, in this case a pimp or bawd

34 *suburban* refers to the locations of the brothels just outside the city of London

bawd woman in charge of a brothel

taffaty taffeta: plain-woven glossy silk

35-7 *like … pig* if they had a bawd Florida and Felecia would charge two pence for admission (like the actors in the public theatres), and the bawd would take most of their wages, leaving them with only one in every ten pennies

37 *the tenth pig* refers to goods taken as tithes, a tax paid to the church). Tithes are sometimes invoked, as here, in the context of sexual share; cf. Webster, *Duchess of Malfi* (1614), ed. John Russell Brown (London: Methuen, 1964): 'I will lie with every woman in my parish the tenth night: / I will tithe them over, like hay-cocks' (4.2.80-1).

42 *beware the buyer* proverbial (Tilley, B788); with a reference to the danger of venereal disease (Leggatt)

44 *whole* with a sexual pun on *hole*: vagina

45 *measure by your own yard* proverbial (Tilley, Y1: 'You measure everyone by your own yard')

yard (1) measurement of distance, equivalent to three feet; (2) penis

46 *Winchester measure* standards for dry and liquid measures were kept at Winchester; Winchester was also associated with the brothels on the Bankside because the area was under the jurisdiction of the bishop of Winchester. Cf. Dekker, *News from Graves-end*: 'O *Winchester!* much mutton hast thou to answer for, which thou hast made away … thy maid servants best know how, if they were cald to account … Oh beware! your *Winchester*-Goose is tenne times more dangerous to surfet upon, than your *S. Nicholas* Shambles-Capon' (B4r).

48 *generating* (1) producing offspring; (2) copulating

sport intercourse

55-6 *you may … oath* smoking and swearing are often represented in Jacobean plays as the stereotypical behaviour of gallants

57 *cuckold-makers* (1) those who have affairs with the wives

of other men (*cuckold*: husband of an unfaithful wife); (2) women themselves, as those who are unfaithful to their husbands

62 *cricket* (1) a chattering woman; cf. Beaumont and Fletcher, *The Coxcomb* (*c.* 1608): 'Lord how shee'le talke some times? tis the maddest cricket –' (4.3.51); (2) relates to the proverbial phrase 'as merry as a cricket' (Tilley C825)

64 *woot* would you

66 *red herring* a dried, smoked herring, which is turned red by the smoke

68 *suit* (1) suit of clothes; (2) 'attendance at court and personal service due from a tenant to his lord; hence used as a formula in describing certain forms of tenure' (*OED* suit *n.* 2 a), leading into Fleer's 'two or three offices' in the next line

70 *offices* jobs, positions of authority

72 *Jurden* chamber-pot

72-3 *Gentleman o'th' Smock* pimp (Williams, 3: 1259); cf. Massinger, *The Maid of Honour* (1621-2), in *The Plays and Poems of Philip Massinger*, ed. Philip Edwards and Colin Gibson, 5 vols (Oxford: Clarendon Press, 1976), vol. 1: 'smocke-agent' (2.2.96)

73 *Smock* shirt-like garment worn as underwear and as night-clothes; emblematic of women's sexual capacity (Williams, 3: 1258-61)

Squire of Entertainment pimp or attendant of prostitutes (Williams, 3: 1298-9)

74 *income* (1) money; (2) entrance

75 *outcome* exit (with pun on *come*: ejaculation)

76 *new-made* recently risen in society

77 *lay … belly* (1) spend everything they have on clothes and food; (2) spend everything on sex (with a sexual pun *spend*: to ejaculate). Cf. Tourneur, *Laugh and Lie Down*

(London, 1605): 'if you have the strength of the backe, you shall not want the necessaries of the Bellie' (sig. B2r; Williams, 1: 52). Related to the proverb 'That which is gotten over the Devil's back is spent under his belly' (Tilley, D316).

79 *musk-cats* (1) civet-cats, from which musk was derived; (2) prostitutes

coop (1) cage; (2) brothel

80 *gallantly* in a gorgeous or showy manner (*OED* gallant *a.* 1a)

81 *court* (1) establishment; (2) law court (picked up in Petoune's reference to the sumner in the next line)

82 *sumner* official who is employed to summon people to appear in court, here also means pimp

85 *calf* fool, sometimes used as a term of endearment (*OED* calf 1c).

a-sucking Petoune has been puffing on his pipe throughout the conversation

87-90 *their … all* (1) their shoes are so elaborate that they can't keep on their feet without assistance, alluding to the exaggerated dress of Venetian courtesans; (2) they are so highly sexed that Fleer has to guide/guard them so that they don't give away their source of income for free. Shoes are a common subject for innuendo, and short heels are often a sign of wantonness; cf. *The Maiden's Tragedy* (*The Second Maiden's Tragedy*), in *Four Jacobean Sex Tragedies*, ed. Martin Wiggins (Oxford: Oxford University Press, 1998): 'Are ye so short-heeled?' (4.1.69) (Williams, 2: 659).

89-90 *play … abroad* behave in the same way outside as at home (*trick*: sexual act)

90 *show all* display their underclothes/genitalia

94 *scoured their pieces* (1) polished their weapons (continuing the military metaphor from ll. 91-2) (2) engaged in

sexual activity with them (*pieces*: genitals)

96 *spend* (1) pay out money; (2) ejaculate, have an orgasm (*OED* spend *v.* 15c). *OED*'s first citation is 1662, but see Sebastian's complex metaphorical story of a 'poppering pear tree' in love with a stream, in which it drops all its fruit, in Tourneur, *The Atheist's Tragedy* (1610-11), in *Four Revenge Tragedies*, ed. Katharine Eisaman Maus (Oxford: Oxford University Press, 1995): 'the poor tree stands as if it were ready to fall and perish by that whereon it spent all the substance it had' (4.1.30, 37-8).
get (1) gain money; (2) contract (an illness) (*OED* get *v.* 14a)

97 *service* (1) employment; (2) sexual action

98-9 *red-nosed corporals* probably alludes to the red nose of Bardolph in *1 Henry IV* (see note to 1.4.116)

100 *whale-nosed* deformed: Williams suggests 'pug-nosed' (2: 958)

101 *snuffle* having a blocked nose, either through a cold or venereal disease (Williams, 3: 1267-8); cf. Dekker, Ford and Rowley, *The Witch of Edmonton* (1621), in *Three Jacobean Witchcraft Plays*, ed. Peter Corbin and Douglas Sedge (Manchester: Manchester University Press, 1986): 'the pox in a snuffling nose is a sign a man is a whore-master' (4.1.39-40)

102 *strikes Petoune* this is apparently the quarrel referred to at the beginning of 3.3, about which Petoune says, ''A struck me, sir, and … had I not taken the box on my cheek, 'a had broke my pipe' (7-10)

103 *fleering* mocking, jeering

104 *cogging* cheating, flattering

105 *hose* article of clothing like stockings or leggings, worn underneath breeches

106 *breech* breeches: trousers that reach just below the knee

107 *French-man's ape* imitation of a French man

109-10 *'Holla .... day?'* quotes Marlowe's *2 Tamburlaine* (*c.* 1589), in *Christopher Marlowe: The Complete Plays*, ed. Mark Thornton Burnett (London: J.M. Dent, 1999): 'Holla, ye pampered jades of Asia! / What, can ye draw but twenty miles a day, / And have so proud a chariot at your heels, / And such a coachman as great Tamburlaine?' (4.3.1-4). The first line is also quoted by the delinquent apprentice Quicksilver in Jonson, Chapman and Marston, *Eastward Ho* (1605), ed. R.W. Van Fossen (Manchester: Manchester University Press, 1979), when he discovers his fellow apprentice, Golding, wooing their master's younger daughter Mildred (2.1.97-8). The sexual connotations may also be relevant in *The Fleer*.

111 *Give ... sun* probably indicates high spirits/ambition (cf. Antifront's reference to Phaeton [1.1.20]), though *bow* can mean male or female genitalia (Williams, 1: 138-9). Leggatt suggests a reference to the 'arrows' scene in *Titus Andronicus* (4.3).

113 *felicity* happiness, bliss (with a possible play on Felecia's name)

115 *light* (1) frivolous; (2) promiscuous

116 *wench* woman or girl

119 *merry* humorous, bawdy

120 *wo't* would (*woot*)

121 *midwife or barber surgeon* those who look after the possible side-effects of Florida and Felecia's trade: unwanted pregnancies and venereal disease

124 *heavy-headed* dull, stupid

127 *pot* drinking vessel (especially for wine or beer)

134-8 *for your louse ... slips from you* comments on the financial and sexual behaviour of the merchant and gentleman: in both respects the merchant is solid and the gentleman slippery

139-41 *they … wenches* either 'they work alongside their wives and spend the money on prostitutes', or 'they prostitute their wives and spend the money on prostitutes'

147 *corks in their shoes* cork soles were popular from the turn of the seventeenth century (Linthicum, p. 242)

149 *light-heeled* (1) light due to the cork; (2) promiscuous

149-51 *The city … actors* cf. Shakespeare, *As You Like It*: 'All the world's a stage, / And all the men and women merely players' (2.7.139-40)

153 *quean* prostitute or otherwise badly behaved woman

155 *cuckold* husband of an unfaithful wife

156 *painter* woman who uses cosmetics (with a swipe at her sexual morality)

157-8 *she … breech* the woman now wears the trousers, i.e. the woman is in control

158-9 *he … feather* a fool is now a gallant (Leggatt)

159-60 *the gentleman … hanger* he is more fashionable (with a probable sexual pun on *long sword/short hanger*: cf. 1.3.53)

161-2 *he … with it* he can now afford to line his cloak with expensive velvet. May also allude to sexual activity – puns on *line*: copulate are common and *velvet* can refer to oral sex – or in particular to adultery; cf. Beaumont and Fletcher, *The Coxcomb*: 'next yeare he will be a velvet-headed Cuckold' (1.5.79-80) (Williams 3: 1470)

164 *meat* (1) food; (2) sexual partners – this play on words is maintained throughout the speech

165-9 *t'one … himself* Leggatt notes the similarity between this sequence and Marston, *The Fawn* (*c.* 1604-5), ed. David Blostein (Manchester: Manchester University Press, 1979): 'These court feasts are to us servitors court fasts; such scambling, such shift for to eat, and where to eat: here a squire of low degree hath got the carcass of a plover, there pages of the chamber divide the spoils of a tattered pheasant, here the sewer has friended a country gentleman with a sweet green goose, and there a young fellow that late has bought his office has caught a woodcock by the nose' (2.1.1-8)

165 *t'one* the one

166 *duck* woman, especially a whore (Williams, 1: 423); cf. Richard Braithwait, *Barnabee's Journal* (London, 1638): 'dainty Ducks … Wenches that could play the wantons' (sig. V1r)

slippery licentious; cf. Shakespeare, *The Winter's Tale* (*c.*1610): 'my wife is slippery?' (1.2.273) (Williams, 3: 1255)

167 *eel* probably signifies a woman (Williams, 1: 431), although Petter argues that this is suggestive of *penis* (a usage also given by Williams) alluding to the polymorphous sexuality of the Jacobean court

tail (1) the train of a woman's dress; (2) genitalia

168 *on't* on it

mumbling (1) chewing or biting softly, as with toothless gums (*OED* mumble *v.* 3); (2) fondling with the lips (*OED* mumble *v.* 4c); (3) mauling (*OED* mumble *v.* 5)

coney (1) rabbit; (2) woman; (3) prostitute

172 *dish* attractive person (*OED* dish *n.* 2a)

173-4 *will ask rich saucing* will cost an extortionate amount (*OED* sauce *v.* 4a). Petter compares Tilley, M839: 'sweet meat must have a sour sauce'; cf. *Eastward Ho*: ''tis no fit sauce for such sweet mutton' (3.2.315-16)

175 *stomach* (sexual) appetite

176 *it* its

kind state, nature

182 *Scot's spur* one of the play's frequent references to the influx of Scottish courtiers in the early years of the reign of James I; it does not seem to refer to any specific fashion. The fact that it is a *fine little Scot's spur* may insinuate that the Scottish courtiers were not well

endowed (I am indebted to Tom Berger for this suggestion).
court jennet a jennet is a small Spanish horse; the court jennet is a courtly lady attracted to the gallant by his up-to-date accessories

183 *curvet* frisk or leap: originally a movement performed by a horse; in this case with sexual innuendo

188 *not a whit* not at all

201 *jack of a clock* the figure that strikes the bell in a clock

206 *courtesans* prostitutes, but often with rich or upper-class clients. *Courtesan* derives from Italian *cortigiana*, feminine of *cortigiano* 'courtier'; Antifront/Fleer plays on the etymology below (ll. 221-3)

210 *o' my word* on my word

211 *stately* arrogant (*OED* stately 2a)

234 *kindness* (1) goodwill; (2) love, sexual affection

236 *nobles* English gold coins, worth 6*s*. 8*d*. in the sixteenth and seventeenth centuries. Four nobles a year would be equivalent to 26*s*. 8*d*. (or £1 6*s*. 8*d*.), a very low wage.

238 *linen* clothes or bed-clothes

247 *blue coats* formerly the uniform of servants, but in the early seventeenth century they were becoming more likely to wear cloaks

248 *kissing of the hand* see note to 1.3.81

273 *sit … courtier* alludes to the infamous sales of titles in the early years of the reign of James I

273-4 *in the presence* in the presence-chamber: the room in which a sovereign receives guests (*OED*)

277-9 *I like … prayers* may refer to the presenting of petitions (Leggatt)

281 *paternoster* the Lord's Prayer, especially the Latin version

284-6 *when … Briton* a reference to the joining of the English and Scottish crowns with the accession of James VI of Scotland to the English throne in 1603; James's plans for political union between the countries were being discussed in Parliament at the time when *The Fleer* was written

290 *statute* law

291 *scores* debts

300 *commodities* goods

305 *strive against the stream* proverbial (Tilley, S592)

311 *But how, I prithee? But* Antifront/Fleer's reply to Ruffle's question may have been censored here (as Leggatt and Petter assume)

312 *hark you* listen

313 *cockatrice* (1) alternative name for a basilisk: a dragon hatched from a cock's egg, which was said to kill with its glance; (2) a prostitute

314 *secrets* sexual organs (*OED* secret *a.* and *n.* 6. *pl.*)

316-17 *I am … trust thee* gallants are constantly in debt to their tailors, who have to trust them to pay for their clothes eventually

324-8 *he … bargain* Antifront/Fleer, as the courtesans' pander, would make less money from them if they were 'private punks' and had fewer clients, and might just as well invest in goods, even insignificant goods such as mouse-traps

342 *procurer* pander: a man who sells women as prostitutes

343 *knave* dishonest or unscrupulous man

352-3 *alchemist … beggar* both of whom try to make gold out of nothing; Petter notes that alchemists were notoriously poor, presumably because their experiments were all unsuccessful

357 *whore-master* a man who uses prostitutes

363 *filcheth* steals

victuals food

364 *flesh* (female) flesh

365 *for't* for it

365-6 *petty larceny* theft of property worth less than 12 pence (*OED*)

367-8 *not … hand* a reference to venereal disease; it will 'burn' Ruffle, but not on the hand, where he would expect to be branded as a convicted criminal

370 *enemies … Jews* Ruffle puns on *gentles* (i.e. gentlemen) and *gentiles* (i.e. non-Jews)

384 *give the Devil his due* give the devil what is owed to him. Proverbial (Tilley, D273).

388 *does … him* in early modern English, inversion of subject and verb in a question can lead to a singular verb followed by a plural subject; cf. Shakespeare, *The Tempest* (*c.* 1611): 'What cares these roarers for the name of King?' (1.1.16-17). See N.F. Blake, *A Grammar of Shakespeare's English* (London: Palgrave, 2002), p. 202.

389 *celestrial* celestial, of the sky. Not found elsewhere; Leggatt argues that it was probably coined by Sharpham to balance 'terrestrial'.

390 *terrestrial* of the earth

392 *gross* (1) material or perceptible to the senses (as opposed to the airy or immaterial) (*OED* gross *a.* 8); (2) coarse or lacking in delicacy (*OED* gross *a.* 11)

element one of the four 'elements' (earth, water, air and fire) which are the natural habitat of any particular class of living beings (*OED* element *n.* 12)

394 *heir* puns on heir/air

395-6 *knighted … sword* refers to the constant creation of knights in the first years of James's reign: a new knight is tapped on both shoulders (or 'dubbed') with a sword

396-7 *lives by the sword* probably a reference to the tendency for needy knights to attempt to woo heiresses (with a pun on *sword*: penis)

403 *beseeched* he beseeched

404-5 *kissed his hand* see note to 1.3.81.

410-11 *extraordinary execution* executions were public events; there may also be a direct reference to the Gunpowder Plot executions of January 1606 (Petter, p. 184)

416 *fleet* shallow (*OED* fleet *a.*^{3} 1), with a possible pun on fleet as a synonym for drain (*OED* fleet *n.*^{2} 1b) if the ladies are crying hypocritically at the execution. The quarto text's *fleet* may be a misprint for *sleet*, as Leggatt argues (Petter wrongly suggests that the text actually reads *sleet* with a long 's'). *Sleet* means *slanting*, but its only recorded use dates from 1440 (*OED* sleet *adv.*).

417 *prospect* view

422-3 *contrary … office* gentleman ushers were supposed to walk in front of their employers

423 *her behind* from behind; *OED*'s first usage of *behind* as a noun dates from 1786 (behind C. *n.* 1)

426 *medlar* fruit resembling a small brown-skinned apple or a human bottom, which are eaten when they have decayed to a softened state; often used in comments on sexuality and moral degeneration

436 *Gravesend* a town in Kent which was the limit of the port of London and the location from which voyages to foreign countries were often started; puns on *grave* as the eventual destination of all people, with the conventional sex/death analogy

437 *tilt-boat* a boat carrying passengers from London to Gravesend; also puns on the sexual associations of *tilt*: cf. Fletcher, *The Woman's Prize* (*c.* 1611): 'and he should tilt her' (3.3.31); Dekker, *Northward Ho* (1605): 'your wife is a Tilt-boate, any man or oman [*sic*] may goe in her for money' (5.1.484-5)

438 *ship yourselves* with a sexual pun on *ship*: (1) vagina; (2) womb; (3) woman (Williams, 3: 1234-5)

444 *e'en* even

446 *confines of Italy* refers to the nationality of Florida and

Felecia

448 *with't* with it

450 *southwards ho!* imitates the calls of boatmen on the Thames; may also allude to three plays performed *c.* 1604-6: Dekker and Webster, *Westward Ho* (Children of Paul's), Jonson, Chapman and Marston, *Eastward Ho* (Children of the Queen's Revels) and Dekker and Webster, *Northward Ho* (Children of Paul's)

451 *storm* puns on *storm*: passion

451-2 *spent their main masts* expended themselves sexually (*mast*: penis)

454 *pomp* splendour

454-5 *under the line … hottest* *line* puns on sexual intercourse and the equator: the 'equatorial line in women's geography means sexual centre' (Williams, 2: 816); cf. Samuel Rowlands, *The Knave of Hearts* (London, 1612), who brings 'pockey news' of a '*whoring Knave*' who has at Lambeth Marsh 'most filthily consorted / With such hot spirited fiery feminine, / That heate him more then underneath the line' (B5r)

460 *decked* adorned, endowed

464 *requite* return

467 *turn* repent, but with a sexual pun (*turn*: to have sex) that undermines the primary meaning; the pun is picked up by Piso in his reply (Williams, 3: 1441)

468-9 *she … now* refers to the habit of turning clothes inside out to make them last longer (Leggatt)

470 *spotted* morally disfigured

475-6 *buzzard … game* buzzards were considered inferior and cowardly by falconers; there may also be an analogy between the hawk presenting its 'tail' and the activities of the courtesans

480 *leer* glance sideways in a lascivious manner

482 *suppositories* solid medical preparations designed to be

inserted into the rectum or vagina to dissolve (*OED*)
glisters enemas

484-5 *like Thisbe … scabbard* he bows so often and so deeply that he has almost impaled himself on his own scabbard; with a sexual *double entendre* (*scabbard*: vagina). Sharpham may refer to the way in which the *Pyramus and Thisbe* sequence in Shakespeare's *A Midsummer Night's Dream* (*c.* 1594) was staged.

492 *honest* chaste

494 *Penelope* wife of Odysseus, who was besieged by suitors during his long absence; she vowed to choose one of them when she had finished weaving a tapestry, but sat up at night unpicking what she had woven during the day so that the task was never finished

504 *needy* poor

506 *lackey* servant

518 *Have a little business* I have a little business

526 *right* birthright

527 *yet would he* yet I would he (i.e. 'I wish he was')

534 *footmen* attendants; originally *running footmen*, servants who ran alongside their master's horse and, later, before their master's carriage (*OED*, footman *n.* 3); *foot* can refer either to the genitals or to copulation, suggesting a bawdy pun here (Williams, 1: 524-5)

537-9 *were … them* servants were often required to run in front of their employers' carriages (Leggatt)

539 *bare* bare-headed

546 *shalt* thou shalt

560 *function* profession

562-6 Sharpham's prose is very like verse here, with internal
574-7 rhymes and some regular iambic pentameter lines (see introduction to Textual Notes)

579 *offices* services, kindness (*OED* office *n.* 1)

583-4 *without imprisonment* without being forced

587 *comely* attractive

611 *occasions calls* in Early Modern English, simple subjects in the plural may have a singular verb; cf. *King Lear*: 'Which very manners urges' (5.3.233) (Blake, *Grammar*, p. 203)

much affection more a lot more affection

617 *deal on use* i.e. act like a usurer

625 *Contemned* treated or regarded with contempt

3.1

8 *nuptial* wedding

13-34 *'Lady … Florence'* the style of the two letters (and the repetition of 'zealous') suggests that the audience is intended to assume that Piso has written both

15 *invocate* call on, invoke

18 *zealous* fervent, enthusiastic

38-9 *a match … revenge* Florida's explosive metaphor would have been topical in early 1606, following the discovery of the Gunpowder Plot in November 1605 (see also note to 2.1.410-11)

44 *Then shall be thus* Then it shall be thus

47 *take the sacrament* swear an oath on a religious symbol; may refer to the Gunpowder Plot conspirators, who were said to have sworn a sacrament (Petter)

53-4 *death and hell stands* see note to 2.1.388

55 *rail* protest strongly, rant

61 *text* proverbial or (especially) scriptural authority (*OED* text *n*. 3). Q1 marks the following line as a sententious phrase (see textual note; cf. 5.3.34).

70-1 *prisoners' box* a box in which inmates of a debtors' prison would solicit charity (money or food) from passers-by (Leggatt, Petter)

71 *ope'* open

74 *arrant* badly behaved

75 *hackney* (1) a horse kept for hire; (2) a prostitute

81 *wast* was it

88-91 *Why … your trade* soldiers were often thought to be lustful; cf. Killigrew, *The Princess, or Love at First Sight* (*c.* 1636), in *Comedies and Tragedies* (London, 1664): 'a Clap is no such dishonour to a Souldier' (sig. G2v)

95-103 Antifront repeats the terms of Piso's rejection of Florida (see 2.1.467-76 and notes)

106 *confusion* destruction (*OED* confusion *n.* 1)

marrow substance found in the centre of bones

115 *physic* medical treatment

116 *ministers to her* looks after her

116-18 *she's … belly* implies that Felecia is pregnant

119-20 *raw fruit* green or unpreserved fruit; cf. *The Duchess of Malfi*: 'This green fruit and my stomach are not friends – / How they swell me!' (2.1.154-5)

121 *plums* linked with the genitals; the homonym *plumb* (a weight attached to the end of a line to measure depth) can also allude to copulation; cf. Markham and Machin, *The Dumb Knight* (*c.* 1607-8; London, 1608): 'What is my wife turnd whore? and must her depth / Be sounded by the plumes of forrainers?' (sig. K1r) (Williams, 3: 1062)

122 *stones* testicles

make her swell Antifront repeats his veiled assertion that Felecia is pregnant; cf. Tourneur, *Laugh and Lie Down*: 'Now fie upon greene Plummes, in troth they make my stomach wamble … But I have met with my breakfast: and therefore I may stay my stomacke to dinner' (sig. F2r)

126-9 *oaten cake … travel well* the sexual *double entendres* on *ride* and *journey*, suggests that oats were an aphrodisiac (Petter). The passage as a whole is likely to satirize King James's Scottish followers.

127 *token* sign of affection (*OED* token *n.* 9)

Sir Ralph Shave *shave* may refer to the loss of hair from syphilis, or to extortion or fleecing (*OED* shave *v.* 7a). The name possibly refers to a popular English perception that Scots were out to cheat them: Petter draws a comparison with Marston's *The Dutch Courtesan* (*c.* 1604-5), ed. David Crane (London: A&C Black, 1997), in which Cockledemoy disguises himself as a 'northern' barber in order to shave (literally and metaphorically) his enemy, Mulligrub the vintner (2.3.13-83).

130 *binder* cause of constipation (*OED* binder 6)

132 *woodcock* (1) a small game-bird; (2) fool (woodcocks were proverbially stupid because they were easy to catch)

133 *You'll go alone* Have-Little will himself be the woodcock, or fool

136 *Under your cloak* Have-Little is the woodcock, so the woodcock will be under his cloak

137 *Mass* by the mass, an expletive

141 *French humour* 'love mad' (Petter); see also note to 1.3.118-19

144 *Tush* an exclamation of disgust or impatience

146 *guarded cloak* a cloak trimmed with braid, lace, velvet, etc.

156-7 *speak … tongue* (1) use all your powers of persuasion; (2) talk about your wealth

158-9 *call … cousin* pretend to a status you do not have

160 *jointure* financial settlement made for the wife in a marriage to provide for her widowhood

161 *warm* amorous (*OED* warm *a.* 13)

168 *God's my life* an expletive

169 *Newcastle* Newcastle-upon-Tyne, Northumbria, from whence London imported coal from the late fourteenth century onwards (Sugden)

172-4 *But … does* his honesty is as non-existent as his money

180 *Aretino's pictures* refers to the notoriously pornographic

illustrations of the Italian poet Pietro Aretino's *Fifteen Days of Marriage*; cf. Jonson, *Volpone* (1605), ed. Philip Brockbank (London: Ernest Benn, 1968): 'for a desperate wit, there's Aretine! / Only, his pictures are a little obscene –' (3.4.96-7)

182 *bawdry* obscenity

186-7 *'John for the King' … 'Up Tails All'* titles of obscene ballads. See H.E. Rollins, ed. *The Pepys Ballads*, 8 vols (Cambridge, MA: Harvard University Press, 1929-1932), 2: 30; William Chappell, *The Ballad Literature and Popular Music of Olden Time*, 2 vols (1885-59; rept. London: Chappell, 1893), 1: 107, 2: 770, 773 (Leggatt, Petter)

190 *Scottish jigs* *jig*: a lively dance, usually in 6/8 time; the 'Scottish jig' may have had a distinctive form and particularly vigorous dance actions (Petter). Here the word *jig* has sexual connotations and implies Felecia's attraction to the incoming Scottish courtiers; cf. Dekker and Webster, *Westward Ho*: 'The Bawde shall teach mee a Scotch Jigge' (5.3.34).

193 *instruments* puns on *instrument*: penis

195 *secretary* a job closer to that of the modern personal assistant than the modern secretary

204 *before* (1) take precedence over; (2) at an earlier point in time. Antifront/Fleer deliberately understands the second meaning in order to mock King James's many new-made knights.

208 *'fore* before

3.2

10 *mare a-nights* night-mare: a *mare* is a goblin which produces bad dreams by sitting on the chest of a sleeper (*OED* mare^2 1)

11 *burst* possibly with a *double entendre* (*burst*: to ejaculate)

14 *clapper* shakes the hopper in a mill so as to make the

grain move down to the millstones (*OED*)

20 *wagtail* profligate or inconstant woman, prostitute

29 *where'er* wherever

33 *reason* intelligence, knowledge

38-40 *make her … lure* Piso turns the negative hawk imagery of 2.1.475-6 and 3.1.102-3 into a positive image of tamed repentance; cf. Shakespeare, *The Taming of the Shrew* (*c.* 1590-3) (4.1.178-95); Fletcher, *The Woman's Prize* (1.2.147-57) and *Rule a Wife and Have a Wife* (1624) (5.3.67-8); Webster, *The Duchess of Malfi* (2.4.28-30)

39 *well-manned* well-trained (Nan picks up the *double entendre*)

40 *lure* device used by falconers to call their hawks back, made of a bunch of feathers with a long cord attached (*OED* lure *n.*[2] 1)

50 *bravery* fine clothes

51 *member* part of the body

52-3 *why … foot* alludes to the proverbial relationship between head and foot ('Do not make the Foot the head' [Tilley, F562]), inverted by Nan in the next line

55 *mechanic* manual labourer or artisan

56 *commonwealth* nation

71 *put 'em to't* don't spare them (Leggatt); cf. Shakespeare, *All's Well That Ends Well* (*c.* 1604): 'Nay, put me to't' (2.2.47)

72 *snick up* go hang (Leggatt); cf. Shakespeare, *Twelfth Night* (1601): 'Sneck up!' (2.3.92)

3.3

9 *trinidado* tobacco imported from Trinidad (*OED*)
box punch

13 *Justice* Justice of the Peace

18-19 *makes him satisfaction* makes amends

30 *ancient* (1) confidant; (2) elderly person; (3) ensign,

standard-bearer: Antifront/Fleer's reply picks up the third sense

32 *colours* (1) flags of a regiment or ship; (2) cosmetics

34-8 *yet … a-work* cf. Thomas Heywood, *The Wise Woman of Hogsden*, ed. Sonia Massai (London: Nick Hern Books, 2003), where the title character runs a brothel and a maternity ward for children born out of wedlock; at 2.1.121 Fleer offers to be as trustworthy as Felecia's 'midwife or barber surgeon'

39 *'tis a good hearing* has a good reputation (*OED* hearing *n.* 3a, 4)

41 *party and party* one side (in a dispute) and the other

47-8 *barber's syringe* used for treating venereal disease

49 *prodigal* spendthrift; wastrel

54 *cozen* cheat

63 *dry hand* lack of sex-drive (due to Fromaga's age)

64 *a very moist nose* like Petoune, Fromaga may be displaying the symptoms of syphilis; the contrast with *dry hand* implies either that Fromaga's sexuality is unaffected by her age, or that she is suffering the effects of an over-active youth

67 *beadles* parish officials with the power to punish petty offenders; here refers to the keepers of Bridewell

68 *Bridewell* London prison, particularly renowned as a place for the punishment of disorderly women; cf. the conclusion of Dekker, *2 The Honest Whore* (*c.* 1605), which is set among the prostitutes in Bridewell

71 *client* (1) hanger-on (*OED* client, *n.* 2a); (2) someone who employs a lawyer (*OED* client, *n.* 3a); customer (*OED* client, *n.* 4a)

73-5 *good … warm* the good client pays money out to the lawyer and gains nothing from it; he is therefore like the lawyer's gown, which keeps the lawyer warm but remains cold itself

77 *puny* junior (*OED* puny *n.* A.1)
clerk scribe of legal documents

77-8 *penny a sheet* a penny per sheet of paper

82 *penny a sheet* a penny per bed-sheet

83 *use* are accustomed

84-96 *There ... often* cf. the similar lists of Portia's suitors in Shakespeare, *The Merchant of Venice* (*c.* 1596) (1.2.35-119), and of Franceschina's clients in Marston, *The Dutch Courtesan*: 'I have made you acquainted with the Spaniard, Don Skirtoll; with the Italian, Master Beieroane; with the Irish Lord, Sir Patrick; with the Dutch merchant, Haunce Herkin Glukin Flapdragon; and specially with the greatest French' (2.2.13-16)

85 *Metheglins* a spiced or medicated variety of mead associated particularly with Wales (*OED*)

86 *Mushroom* Sharpham may assume that Frenchmen are particularly susceptible to women: in *The Atheist's Tragedy*, Tourneur associates mushrooms with female sexuality: 'The love of a woman is like a mushroom: it grows in one night and will serve somewhat pleasingly next morning to breakfast, but afterwards waxes fulsome and unwholesome' (4.5.30-3). It may also refer to the nouveau riche, who proverbially spring up overnight like mushrooms, or to something worthless; cf. Jonson, *The Poetaster* (1601), ed. Tom Cain (Manchester: Manchester University Press, 1995): 'a mushroom for all your other ornatures' (3.1.55-6).

87 *Fumada* refers to smoked pilchards (*fumade*), particularly associated with Spain; cf. Dekker (?), *Blurt Master Constable* (1601; London, 1602): 'What meate eates the *Spaniard*?'/ 'Dry'd *pilchars* and poore John' (sig. B3v) (Leggatt, Petter)

88 *Usquebaugh* whisky, derived from the Gaelic 'water of life'

90 *Slopdragon* a conflation of two stereotypical Dutch attributes. (1) *flapdragon*, a drinking game in which raisins placed in lighted brandy are caught in the players' mouths and eaten (can also refer to the raisin itself). Associated in particular with the Dutch; cf. Barry, *Ram Alley* (*c.* 1608; London, 1611): 'my brother swallows it with more ease then a Dutchman does flap-Dragons' (sig. C3v). (2) Baggy 'slops' were a standard article of Dutch dress (Sugden, Leggatt).

92 *Saluberrimum* 'most healthful' in Latin (Leggatt)

94 *Rowel* a spiked revolving disc on the end of a spur

95 *Tower Hill* area to the north of the Tower of London

97 *deal* (1) engage in combat (*OED* deal *v.* 10); (2) have sex (*OED* deal *v.* 11b)

chambers (1) pieces of ordinance; (2) rooms

97-100 *as well … Westminster* when the Lord Mayor came to Westminster to meet the King after his investiture, a salute was fired from Lambeth (Sugden, s.v. Lambeth)

99-100 *Lambeth … Westminster* Lambeth is an area south of the river Thames, where the Archbishop of Canterbury's London residence was located; it is directly across the river from Westminster, site of the royal palace and the seat of government

102 *sack* dry white wine

4.1

1-5 *Health… Spark* cf. *Hamlet*, where Claudius addresses 'Rosencrantz and gentle Guildenstern' and Gertrude addresses 'Guildenstern and gentle Rosencrantz' (2.2.33-4)

9 *sconce* head, with a pun on its alternative meaning of fortification (*OED* sconce *n.* 3)

14-19 *And … fair* Petoune's speech anatomises Fromaga's body as landscape: the Alps represent her breasts, the 'narrow passage' her vagina, and the 'towering head of high mount Chiego' her *mons veneris* (Leggatt)

17 *mount Chiego* a mountain on the coast of Spain at the entrance to the straits of Gibraltar (Sugden, s.v. Gibraltar)

19 *passing* very (*OED* passing *adv*. a)

26 *muff* used as an expression of disgust

28 *God's me* God save me: an expletive

30-1 *the moon … change* a reference to the supposed changeability of women, often compared with the waxing and waning of the moon

32-3 *know me … kindness* be more kind to me

35 *flirts* giddy young women

some other where somewhere else

39 *tempering of colours* preparing cosmetics

drawn-work ornamental needlework done by drawing out some of the threads so as to form patterns

46 *I'll take you down* I'll get the better of you (with a sexual pun)

47 *simpering* coy, coquettish

76 *lines* the words of Have-Little's letter (see 3.1.13-21)

89 *durst you* would you dare

92 *my soul's eternity* the immortality of my soul

114-16 *First … secure* These lines could be treated as verse, since the metre is reasonably regular and there is an internal rhyme (Petter lines 115-16 as verse)

115 *t'enjoy* to enjoy

123-7 *Let … I'll do't* Piso's lines could be treated as (somewhat irregular) blank verse; the language and syntax parody the excesses of Jacobean revenge tragedy

129 *hap* happens

132 *means* method

136 *give them a fig* (1) poison them (proverbial, deriving from the practice of poisoning figs [Tilley, F213]); (2)

insult them (*a fig* is a contemptuous gesture in which the thumb is thrust between two closed fingers or into the mouth [*OED* fig *n.*[2]])

141 *a health* a toast

142 *mingle* mix

dram a measure equivalent to one eighth of a fluid ounce, used figuratively to denote a small amount of liquid, often of a spirit or medicine (*OED* dram *n.*[1] 3a)

143 *in post* with haste, quickly

145 *breed suspect* cause suspicion

148 *well stored* has a good stock

158 *pieces* women (pieces of flesh) (*OED* piece *n.* 3c)

168 *fiddlers* sexual partners (Williams, 1: 480)

169 *instruments* see note to 3.1.191

173 *curtals* (1) animals with their tails docked, especially horses (*OED* curtal *n.* 1-3); (2) a kind of bassoon (*OED* curtal *n.* 5, continuing Antifront/Fleer's musical metaphor); (3) whores (*OED* curtal *n.* 3d)

186 *span-counter* a game in which the players throw counters, the second player aiming either to hit their opponent's counter or to get their counter so near it that they can span the space with their hand and touch both the counters

188 *drink drunk* drink until I get drunk

lie tell falsehoods; with a *double entendre* on *lie*: to have sex with

189 *lackey* servant, with a possible pun on *lack*

191 *puny* junior (see note to 3.3.77)

194 *all* all the stories

197 *common* sexually available

as common as a proverbial construction (Tilley, B73, C109, H457, C509 etc.)

200 *the operation of the pot* drinking

203 *complain them* complain about them

4.2

1 *eryngo* candied root of sea holly (an aphrodisiac)

3 *concoct* heat, boil

6 *civet* a musk-like substance derived from the sac or glands of the civet cat, used in perfumery

12 *young pups* *pup* a contemptuous term for a foolish young man. Q1 reads 'poops': I follow Petter, who comments that the *young pups* 'would smell the *civet*'. Nibbe and Leggatt gloss poops as 'farts', but this seems an odd combination with *young*.

14 *bushels* measures of capacity equivalent to four pecks or eight gallons

16 *quintessence* essential part, purest form

19 *degree* rank

20 *I … so* I could never manufacture it so well

22 *what do ye lack* traditional call of tradesmen

39 *liberal* generous

41 *Jacques* French form of Giacomo

45 *am fitted for* can pass for

S'heart God's heart: an expletive

52 *lotiums* cosmetic treatments for the hair, normally made from stale urine

restringent restraining the action of the bowels (*OED*)

53 *aqua mirabilis* water distilled with spirit wine, cloves, mace, nutmeg, ginger and other spices (*OED*)

cordial stimulating, comforting or invigorating

54 *receipts* preparations or remedies

67 *a cat hath nine lives* proverbial (Tilley, C154)

80 *good service* (1) good work; (2) good sex

83 *French crown* English term for the French *ecu*, regarded as equivalent to the English crown

4.3

6 *shalt* thou shalt

9-10 *jet … thither* jet can attract light objects if it is electrified by rubbing; cf. Jonson, *Every Man in his Humour* (1598, rev. 1616): 'Draw courtship to you as a jet doth straws' (ed. Miola, Appendix I, 3.3.21)

11-13 *springle … affections* proverbial (Tilley, S788: 'a springle to catch a woodcock'); see also note to 3.1.132; cf. Shakespeare, *Hamlet*: 'springes to catch woodcocks' (1.3.115), also referring to sexuality

11 *springle* spring or snare

14 *commodity* something useful or advantageous

16 *discommodity* something unsuitable or disadvantageous

16-17 *the heat of blood in youth* sexual urges of young men (cf. 'hot-blooded')

18 *but on a scab* may refer to a symptom of syphilis, one of the possible results of the 'heat of blood in youth'

5.1

1-12 *Oh … nations* It is not clear whether Petoune attended the banquet, and, if he did, how he survived; tobacco was supposed to protect the smoker from poison (Pollard).

11-12 *law of nations* civil or Roman law as opposed to the English common law

116 *sentinels* guards

5.2

3 *are you towards him* do you serve him

25 *yield good aspect* look favourably

5.3

1-34 For the first time since 1.1, Sharpham writes an entire scene in blank verse.

5 *burthen* burden

17 *liberality* generosity

22 *untemperate* intemperate

25 *fatness* fertility

28 *the mean's … music* a moderate life is best: *mean* is the middle or intermediate part in musical harmony (*OED* mean *a.*^{2} 1b)

34 *None … sin* marked as a sententious phrase in Q1 (see textual note; cf. 3.1.61)

5.4

6-7 *as long … ended* a comment on the slow progress of a legal case through the courts

9 *As broad … bill* hell was a slang term for a debtors' prison; debt was a matter that could be handled by the Court of Chancery (Leggatt). Therefore, being in debt and being sued at Chancery would take you to hell.

11 *on't* on it

13 *were't* were it

18-20 *they'll … sponges* they'll drink even more than a Dutch captain and (absorb) more than a sponge. English stereotype held that the Dutch were particularly heavy drinkers (Sugden). On 'court ladies' sponges' cf. Jonson, *Epicoene* (1609), ed. R.V. Holdsworth (London: Ernest Benn, 1979): 'There's no man can be admitted till she be ready nowadays … but the boy here, and him she wipes her oiled lips upon like a sponge' (1.1.81-5).

22 *four sons of Aymon* heroes of romance, and the subjects of a play performed by the Admiral's Men in 1603 (R.A. Foakes and R.T. Rickert, eds., *Henslowe's Diary: Edited with Supplementary Material, Introduction and Notes* [Cambridge: Cambridge University Press, 1961], pp. 208, 211)

26 *apes* imitators

29-68 *Yes … gratis* the damned souls described by Spark and Ruffle have all been paradoxically condemned to hell for not indulging in the sins typical of Londoners

30 *desperate debt* a bad debt

34 *mercenary woman* prostitute (see note to 2.1.19)

35 *puritan* (1) an English Protestant who thought that the Elizabethan reformation of the church was incomplete and argued for its further 'purification' (*OED* puritan *n.* 1); (2) someone who either is or pretends to be extremely strict in their religion or morals (*OED* puritan *n.* 2)

40 *painted* used cosmetics: the use of cosmetics is frequently linked with female transgression. In Barnabe Barnes' *The Devil's Charter* (*c.* 1606) the evil Lucretia Borgia is poisoned with her own cosmetics.

40-1 *puritan … eyes* Leggatt compares *How a Man May Choose a Good Wife From a Bad* (*c.* 1602), ed. A.E.H. Swaen (Louvain: A. Uystpruyst / London: David Nutt, 1912): in which a hypocritical puritan woman 'seeming divine, turnd up the white of eye' (sig. G3r)

41-2 *a tailor … fingers* probably alludes to the proverbial lasciviousness of tailors (Williams, 3: 1358-9); cf. Dekker and Webster, *Northward Ho*: 'Tailors wilbe sawcie and lickerish' (2.1.177); Sharpham, *Cupid's Whirligig* (1607; London, 1607): 'You are like a mans Taylor that workes with open shop for the Husband, but if you have a chance to doe any thing for the wife, you must doe it inwards, inwards!' (sig. B4v)

42 *scabby* may allude to the pox, though Leggatt suggests that it is used figuratively

42-3 *a vintner … sugar* tapsters sold small packets of sugar to sweeten dry wine (Leggatt); the tapster is damned for *not* giving short measures to his customers

49 *For … purse* refers to the stereotypical poverty of (spendthrift) Inns of Court students

52 *benchers* senior members of the Inns of Court

53 *angels* (1) heavenly creatures; (2) gold nobles (coins

worth 6*s*. 8*d*.) bearing the picture of the Archangel Michael

67 *scrivener* receives money to place out at interest and supplies those who want to raise money on security (*OED*, scrivener *n.* 3)

71 *gossiping* festive; baptismal (*gossips* are godparents)

Proserpina Roman name for Persephone, the daughter of Ceres/Demeter and wife of Pluto/Hades; Sharpham mixes classical and biblical tradition, and marries Proserpina to the devil

74 *sergeant and a yeoman* officials in a royal household, the yeoman ranking between a sergeant and a groom (*OED* yeoman I.1; sergeant *n*. 7)

75 *to nurse* to a wet-nurse

77 *counter in Wood Street* a prison in the City of London; a counter is a prison for debtors (Leggatt, Sugden s.v. Wood Street)

78 *slaves … horse-leeches* probably refers to the profits made by officials exploiting their prisoners (Leggatt)

5.5

0.1 SD *Doctor CAIUS* Caius and the other judges are Doctors of Law

25-6 *in this sort* in this manner, in these circumstances

29 *footed* kept step with (*OED* foot *v*. 1a)

29-30 *like … measure* like an inexperienced dancer failing to keep step

31 *unbacked* untrained, unbroken

wanton unruly; skittish (especially when used of an animal – see *OED* wanton *a*. 1b)

35-6 *so … as* so … that

36 *overset* capsized

barque a small ship

42 *surfeited* glutted

51 *divers* several
52 *drenched* administered
53-4 *discharge the debt they owed to nature* die
59-60 *the weaker vessels* a proverbial metaphor for the supposed inferiority of women (Tilley, W655)
69 *hand* handwriting
74 *upon this hand* by the authority of this handwriting
123 *satisfaction* recompense
126-39 The play's conclusion parodies the endings of other 'disguised ruler' narratives such as *Measure for Measure* and *The Malcontent*
127 *I … word* I hold you to your word (Leggatt)

SYNOPSIS

The action of *The Fleer* begins in Florence, where Antifront has been deprived of his dukedom by the usurping Lord Piso; Antifront's daughters, Florida and Felecia, have fled. Antifront disregards the council of one of his lords and decides to disguise himself in order to search for his lost children. The action then moves to London, where it remains for the rest of the play; the milieu is self-consciously comedic, mingling gallants, whores, and girls disguised as boys, and Sharpham works in a number of set-piece comic scenes, mostly dialogues involving Antifront in his dyspeptic disguise-persona, Fleer.

The second and third scenes focus on Florida and Felecia, Antifront's daughters, who on reaching London have gone into business as prostitutes (or, as Felecia prefers, courtesans). They regret that they have been forced to lower themselves from the expectations their high birth has bred in them, but reason that they have no other way of making a living, invoking specious *carpe diem* arguments to assuage their guilty consciences. The next scene introduces Fromaga, Florida and Felecia's elderly waiting gentlewoman (and, Sharpham implies, their bawd). Fromaga interviews a would-be gentleman usher who has been recommended to them by Sir John Have-Little, she then introduces him to Florida and Felecia.

The malignant Florida and Felecia are balanced by two more sisters, Nan and Susan, witty London citizens who are in love with the gallants Spark and Ruffle. Spark and Ruffle, accompanied by Have-Little and Piso – the son of the Florentine usurper – introduce the sisters to Petoune, a foolish gallant who is addicted to tobacco. In a comic set-piece, Petoune humiliates himself by offering Susan an empty pipe, and is forced to swear on the same pipe that he will abjure the sisters' company.

After Petoune's retreat, Antifront enters in his disguise as Fleer and Spark offers to prefer him to the service of Florida and Felecia, not knowing that he is in fact their father. Nan and Susan decide to disguise themselves as boys and become Spark and Ruffle's servants, in order to prevent them from marrying other women and eventually win their love.

In a monologue at the start of Act 2, Antifront despairs at the behaviour of his daughters but reveals that he is acting as their pander; he comments satirically about the inhabitants of London. In other exchanges, Florida and Felecia debate their reputation with Antifront, and Antifront, Ruffle and Spark swap jokes about courtiers, sexual morality and current events (including the debate over the Union of Britain and the behaviour of women at executions). Antifront tries to draw Florida to Piso's attention, and urges Felecia's case with Have-Little; he hopes that marriage will reform his daughters, but also that through Florida's marriage to Piso his family can regain their status in Florence. Have-Little is amenable, but Piso pours scorn on Florida's sexual mores. Susan and Nan's attempt to enter Ruffle and Spark's service is unsuccessful, and they are instead taken on by Piso and Have-Little. Meanwhile, Piso begins to fall in love with Florida. Florida and Felecia woo Spark and Ruffle, and, rejected, plot their revenge.

At the opening of Act 3 Florida and Felecia compare love-letters they have received from Have-Little and Piso, and decide to persuade them to murder Spark and Ruffle. They are overheard, however, by Antifront. After Florida and Felecia's departure, Piso despairs about his love for Florida and bridles at Antifront's teasing; he confides in Nan, who advises him to try to win her love by neglecting her. Petoune reveals his love for Fromaga, and asks Antifront's advice on how to woo her: they rehearse a serious of parodic compliments.

When they meet, at the start of Act 4, Petoune's blandishments win Fromaga over and she agrees to marry him. Florida and Felecia persuade Piso and Have-Little to poison Spark and Ruffle at a banquet, and Piso volunteers to buy the poison from Alunio, a

Florentine apothecary. They are again overheard by Antifront, now accompanied by Nan and Susan. Antifront realises that the sisters are women in disguise, but agrees not to reveal them; they plan to prevent the murders. In the next scene, Alunio the apothecary is about to leave for Florence, and is glad to hand his shop over to Antifront, who claims to be an unemployed apothecary. Antifront sells Piso and Have-Little an innocuous sleeping potion instead of the poison they intend to buy.

At the start of Act 5, Petoune tells Nan the news that Ruffle and Spark have died at a banquet held by Piso and Have-Little; the hosts have been arrested and are to be tried for the murders. Antifront is sent to fetch Justice Ferrio, the chief judge; Ferrio is sick, however, and sends his ring to the court, asking Judge Caius to act in his stead. In another comic interlude, Spark and Ruffle tell Antifront about their experiences in 'hell', another opportunity for Sharpham to present a discussion about contemporary London. At the trial, Antifront appears before the court in the guise of a judge, telling Caius that he has been authorised by Ferrio to act on his behalf. He presents a letter written by 'Fleer', which accuses Florida and Felecia. The sisters repent, and declare their love for Have-Little and Piso. At that moment a messenger from Florence appears, telling Piso that his father is dead and he is now Duke; Piso asks them to call back Duke Antifront, vowing to marry his eldest daughter and restore him to his estates. On these words, Antifront reveals himself, calls in the revived Spark and Ruffle, and pairs off the cast: Piso and Florida, Have-Little and Felecia, Spark and Nan, Ruffle and Susan, and Petoune and Fromaga. The play ends with a conventional plea for applause.

TEXTUAL NOTES

The Fleer was first published in 1607, in a quarto edition printed by Edward Allde and sold by Francis Burton (hereafter Q1). The play had been entered in the Stationers' Register on 13 May 1606 (to John Trundell and John Busbye on the condition that they bring 'good aucthoritie and licence for Doinge thereof') and transferred on 12 November 1606 to John Busbye and Arthur Johnson. W.W. Greg's conviction that the first edition 'was clearly not produced in pursuance of the entry in the SR' (*A Bibliography of the English Printed Drama to the Restoration* [London: Bibliographical Society, 1939], 1: 387) is perhaps overstated. Arthur Johnson was the publisher of Sharpham's second play, *Cupid's Whirligig*, and he and Francis Burton collaborated on other projects.

Three further editions were issued, all published by Nathaniel Butter: 1610 (hereafter Q2), printed by Thomas Purfoot; 1615 (hereafter Q3), for which the printer has not been positively identified; and 1631 (hereafter Q4), printed by Bernard Alsop and Thomas Fawcett. In addition, ten of the play's jokes were recycled in Robert Chamberlain's jest-book, *Conceits, Clinches, Flashes and Whimzies* (1639), and five extracts of varying lengths were reprinted in John Cotgrave's *The English Treasury of Wit and Language* (1655). Aside from these items, the play's textual history is fairly clear: Q1 is the only text with which the author could have been involved, since he died in April 1608; Q2 was printed directly from Q1, with some minor corrections, and Q3 from Q2, with further corrections. Q4 adopts some but not all of Q3's changes; some of the text seems to have been set from Q1 or Q2 and the remainder from Q3 (see Christopher Gordon Petter, *A Critical Old-Spelling Edition of the Works of Edward Sharpham* [New York: Garland, 1986], pp. 236-7).

Q1, the only edition with any claim to authority, is a clean and generally well-produced text, and it seems likely that the author was involved in its publication, despite the reference to his absence from London in the prefatory letter 'To the Reader and Hearer'. The only recurring problem is with speech-headings, where the conjunction of *Fleire* (*Fle.* or *Fl.*), *Florida* (*Flo.* or *Fl.*), and *Felecia* (*Fel.*) seems to have confused the compositors. Some corrections have been made in press (see Petter, pp. 237-9). It is likely that some sections of the text have been censored, as noted in the Editor's Introduction, but none of the possible excisions disrupt the sense very much, and probably would not be noticed in performance (see Glossarial Note for 2.1.311).

Later editions of *The Fleer* comprise Hunold Nibbe's edition for W. Bang's series *Materialien zur Kunde des älteren englischen Dramas* (London: David Nott, 1912), and Petter's *Critical Old Spelling Edition of the Works of Edward Sharpham* (1986). Nibbe's edition is a transcript of Q1, apparently based on British Library 11773.c.8, with substantial textual and glossarial notes. Petter's text is an old-spelling edition with full textual apparatus and critical commentary; he collates six copies of Q1 (British Library, John Rylands, Huntington, Yale, Folger and Harvard), using Yale as his copy-text, and he also provides a collation of Q1-4.

The text of this edition has been fully modernised, and abbreviations have been silently expanded. Readings proposed by Nibbe and Petter have been considered, and in some cases adopted. I have also consulted Alexander Leggatt's unpublished MA thesis, 'The Plays of Edward Sharpham: An Introduction and a Commentary' (University of Birmingham, 1963). For this edition of *The Fleer* a full collation has not been attempted (in line with Globe Quartos editorial procedures), but the copy-text (British Library 11773.c.8) has been checked against Petter's collations. When adopted, Petter's readings have been checked against copies of Q1-4 in the British Library and against those available on *Early English Books Online* (http://eebo.chadwyck.com).

Problems are caused by Sharpham's occasional use of verse, which is notably irregular and is often printed as prose in Q1-4.

Where necessary it has been relined, notably in 1.1 and 5.3. In other places (e.g. 2.1.574-7, 632-5) I have decided to leave speeches as prose throughout; picking out isolated verse lines would leave the speeches looking disjointed and might place undue emphasis on these lines.

As noted above, some of the speech-heads are clearly incorrect, and they have been amended. I have also chosen to refer to Antifront/Fleer as Antifront throughout: to use two names would cause unnecessary confusion and it seems odd to refer to the character as Fleer in 1.1, before he has taken on his disguise. Q1 has act divisions but no scene divisions (see textual notes for 2.1, 3.1, 4.1 and 5.1); I have generally followed Petter's division of scenes, but have inserted a new scene at 1.3. Stage directions in square brackets are editorial; some are based on Petter but others are new.

Particular problems are caused by some idiosyncrasies in the text. In *The Fleer*, *a* is used frequently for *s/he*; as Stanley Wells notes, there is 'no wholly satisfactory way of representing this typographically' since all of the alternatives (*'e*, *a* or *'a*) are problematic (*Modernizing Shakespeare's Spelling* [Oxford: Clarendon Press, 1979], p. 26). Wells decides that retaining the original text's *a* is the best solution. This risks confusion, however, and I have therefore decided, *pace* Wells, to follow the example of Nicola Bennett's Globe Quartos edition of *The Merry Devil of Edmonton* (London: Nick Hern Books, 2000) and have used *'a* throughout this edition.

Similarly, I have substituted *'em* for Q1's *'am*. Both are variations on the unstressed form of *hem*; *OED* notes, 'The emphatic form of the pronoun was early superseded by THEM, but the unstressed form continued to be used, being regarded as an abbreviation of them.' I have used *'em* throughout this edition to avoid confusion with *am* as a form of the verb *to be*.

Another problem is posed by the text's use of the elision *pra'y*, meaning *pray ye*, for which there seems to be no fully satisfactory modernisation. The best solution seems to be to use *pray 'e* (suggested by Gabriel Egan), which conveys the right sound to the reader and/or performer.

Following the example of Roger Warren's recent edition of *Cymbeline*, I have modernised *Iacomo* (the name used by Antifront/Fleer in 4.2) to its closest modern equivalent, *Giacomo* (see *Cymbeline*, ed. Roger Warren [Oxford: Oxford University Press, 1998], pp. 102, 268).

Sources referred to

Q1 – 1607
Q1(u) – Q1 uncorrected
Q1(c) – Q1 corrected
Q2 – 1610
Q3 – 1615
Q4 – 1631
Nibbe – Hunold Nibbe, ed., *The Fleire*, Materialien zur Kunde des älteren englischen Dramas (London: David Nott, 1912)
Leggatt – Alexander Leggatt, 'The Plays of Edward Sharpham: An Introduction and a Commentary', unpublished MA thesis, University of Birmingham, 1963
Petter – Christopher Gordon Petter, *A Critical Old Spelling Edition of the Works of Edward Sharpham* (New York: Garland, 1986)

Abbreviations

this edn – readings original to or first accepted in this edition
SD – Stage Direction
SP – Speech Prefix
( ) – suggested but not adopted by a previous commentator

Numbering of SDs and SPs follows Bennett, ed., *The Merry Devil of Edmonton*. SDs and SPs take the number of the line in which they appear. Line references including a decimal point, such as 60.1-2, refer to entry SDs. Entry SDs at the beginning of scenes are numbered 0.1, 0.2 etc. In both cases the number after the decimal point refers to the line within the SD.

1.1

1-29	Dear Lord … *sorte*] *prose Q1; verse Petter*
26	disguisement is too great] *this edn;* disguisement is to great *Q1*

1.2

1.1	SD] *this edn; Exeunt all but the two Sisters Q1*
11	to seek] *Q3-4;* seeke *Q1-2*
24-5	No, no, not I ... I'll die] *prose Q1; verse Petter*
26	resolutions] *Q1;* resolution *Petter*
31-3	and though ... Florence] *prose Q1; verse Petter*
34	SP]*Q3, Petter; om. Q1-2, 4*
	SD] *this edn; om. Q1*

1.3

0	Scene division] *this edn*
0.1-2	SD] *this edn; Enter Fromaga, and Ladyes Exeunt. To her enter a Gentleman. Q1*
3	SD] *Petter; om. Q1*
5	SD] *Nibbe, Petter; om. Q1*
	'A] *this edn;* a *Q1 (see discussion above)*
9	'em] 'am *Q1 (see discussion above)*
10	'em] 'am *Q1 (see discussion above)*
15	'a] *this edn;* a *Q1 (see discussion above)*
28	pin] *Q1; Nibbe glosses* pin *as pencil; Leggatt writes, 'read* pen'
42	wear] *this edn;* weare *Q4, Petter;* were *Q1-3*
46	his] *Q1-2, 4;* her *Q3, Petter;* their *(Leggatt)*
53	hangers of your] *Q1-2, 4;* hangers your *Q3, Petter*

64 hour] houre *Q2-4, Petter;* honre *Q1*
74 SD] *this edn; om. Q1*
78 SD] *this edn; om. Q1*
81 SD] *this edn; om. Q1*
82.1-2 SD] *this edn; Deliuers a Letter Q*
83 have read it] Q; and have read it *(Leggatt)*
89 inn's court] Innes Court *Q1-2, 4;* Innes of Court *Q3, Petter*
91 gentleman] *Q3-4;* Gent. *Q1-2*
99 and must] *Q1-2, 4;* and you must *Q3*
109 'a] *this edn;* a *Q1 (see discussion above)*
110 'a] *this edn;* a *Q1 (see discussion above)*
114 'a] *this edn;* a *Q1 (see discussion above)*
'a] *this edn;* a *Q1 (see discussion above)*
116 'a] *this edn;* a *Q1 (see discussion above)*
123 pray 'e] *this edn;* pra'y *Q1 (see discussion above)*
130 't 'as] *this edn;* t'as Q1
134 SD] *this edn; om. Q1*
'a] *this edn;* a *Q1 (see discussion above)*
140 'a] *this edn;* a *Q1 (see discussion above)*
141 'a] *this edn;* a *Q1 (see discussion above)*

1.4

10-12 O had ... thine] *verse Petter; prose (italic) Q1*
16-17 O be ... rough] *verse Petter; prose (italic) Q1*
18 'a] *this edn;* a *Q1 (see discussion above)*
19 'a] *this edn;* a *Q1 (see discussion above)*
'a] *this edn;* a *Q1 (see discussion above)*
20 'a] *this edn;* a *Q1 (see discussion above)*
28-31 'Spare ... swim'] *this edn; italics Petter; roman type Q1*
32-3 'By my ... everything'] *this edn; italics Petter; roman type Q1*
46 his soul's] his *Q4;* so *Q1-3*
48-9 His discourse ... felicity] *prose Q1; verse Petter*

50 SD] *this edn; om. Q1*
Pray] *this edn;* Pray' *Q1*
51 SD] *this edn; om. Q1*
55 SD] *this edn; om. Q1*
56 SD] *this edn; om. Q1*
62.1-2 SD] *this edn; Enter Spark, Ruffell, Piso, Knight, and Petoune Q1*
84 a-mornings] *Q3;* mornings] *Q1-2, 4*
97 'a] *this edn;* a *Q1 (see discussion above)*
'a] *this edn;* a *Q1 (see discussion above)*
98 'a] *this edn;* a *Q1 (see discussion above)*
112 gentlemen] *Nibbe, Petter*; Gentlewomen *Q1*
119 'a] *this edn;* a *Q1 (see discussion above)*
121 'a] *this edn;* a *Q1 (see discussion above)*
'a] *this edn;* a *Q1 (see discussion above)*
123 gentlemen] *Nibbe, Petter*; Gentlewomen *Q1*
126 SD] *this edn; om. Q1*
136 'a] *this edn;* a *Q1 (see discussion above)*
'a] *this edn;* a *Q1 (see discussion above)*
138 SD] *this edn; om. Q1*
140 pray 'e] *this edn;* pra'y *Q1 (see discussion above)*
141 know it] *Q2-4;* know tit *Q1*
172 gentlemen] *Nibbe, Petter;* Gentlewomen *Q1*
177 SD] *this edn; om. Q1*
179-80 SD] *this edn;* (tab) *Q1;* [RUFFEL *takes a few draughts and discovers the pipe to be empty of tobacco*] *Petter.*
Q's (tab) *seems to be a stage direction, and an abbreviation for 'tabaco', but for the reader of the play it may also have read as an in-joke, since 'tabe' or 'tabes' is a gradual wasting away caused by disease (OED)*
191 nobody] *this edn;* no bodie *Q1 (c);* no bo bodie *Q1 (u)*
193 'a] *this edn;* a *Q1 (see discussion above)*
is good] *Q1(c);* good is *Q1(u)*
195 SD] *this edn; om. Q1*

199 in anything] in anything *Q1(c);* iv anything *Q1(u)*
207 SD] *this edn; om. Q1*
208 SD] *this edn; om. Q1*
211 SD] *this edn; om. Q1*
218 SD] *this edn; om. Q1*
224 Most] *Q1(c);* Nost *Q1(u)*
225 'a] *this edn;* a *Q1 (see discussion above)*
232 SD] *this edn; om. Q1*
257 SD] *this edn; om. Q1*
259 SD] *this edn; om. Q1*
267 God be w'ye] *Petter;* God bewe *Q1*
270 SD] *Petter; Exit Q1*
293 SD] *Nibbe, Petter; om. Q1*
298 'a] *this edn;* a *Q1 (see discussion above)*
347.1-3 SD] *this edn; Exeunt. | manent Su, Nan Q1*; *Q1 places SD in margins of 346-7*
348-52 Come ... wives] *prose Q1; verse Petter*

2.1

0 [Act 2, Scene 1]] *this edn*; *Finis Actus Primi. / Actus secundus. Q1*
0.1 SD] *this edn*; *Enter Fleire, Solus in a new Suite.Q1*
14 'a] *this edn;* a *Q1(see discussion above)*
15 'a] *this edn;* a *Q1(see discussion above)*
'a] *this edn;* a *Q1(see discussion above)*
16 'a] *this edn;* a *Q1(see discussion above)*
'a] *this edn;* a *Q1(see discussion above)*
23 friar] *Nibbe, Petter;* Fryers *Q1*
27 'em] *this edn;* a'm *Q1 (see discussion above)*
28 'em] *this edn;* a'm *Q1 (see discussion above)*
34 suburban] *this edn;* suburbian *Q1*
'em] *this edn;* am *Q1 (see discussion above)*
62 cricket] *Q3;* crickee *Q1-2, 4*
95 very] *Q4;* wee *Q1-2; om. Q3*

102 SD] *this edn; om. Q1*

104.1-2 SD] *this edn; Enter two ladies, one singing: Q1*

110 can] *Q2-4*; ean *Q1*

121 SP] *this edn*; *Flo: Q1*; FLEIRE *Petter*

123 SP] *this edn*; *Flo: Q1*; FLEIRE *Petter*

124 heavy-headed] heauie headed *Q3*; heauie head *Q1-2, 4*

138 'a] *this edn;* a *Q1 (see discussion above)*

144 'A] *this edn;* A *Q1 (see discussion above)*

210 o'] *this edn;* a' *Q1*

213 'em] *this edn;* am *Q1 (see discussion above)*

220 pray 'e] *this edn;* pra'y *Q1 (see discussion above)*

224 SD] *this edn; om. Q1*

227 'em] *this edn;* am *Q1 (see discussion above)*

230 SD] *Petter; om. Q1*

239 'a] *this edn;* a *Q1 (see discussion above)*

247 off] *Q3-4;* oft *Q1-2*

267.1 FLORIDA *and* FELECIA] *this edn; Sisters Q1*

267.2 *in fine clothes*] *this edn; om. Q1*

276-7 Oh ... game] *prose Q1; verse Petter*

301 but to try thee] but to trie *Q1;* but trie *Petter*

327 'a] *this edn;* a *Q1 (see discussion above)*

339 'em] *this edn;* am *Q1 (see discussion above)*

354 pray 'e] *this edn;* pra'y *Q1 (see discussion above)*

359 SD] *Petter; om. Q1*

'a] *this edn;* a *Q1 (see discussion above)*

360 SD] *this edn; [To him] Petter; om. Q1*

365-6 petty larceny] *this edn;* pettilassarie *Q1*

376 'a] *this edn;* a *Q1 (see discussion above)*

'a] *this edn;* a *Q1 (see discussion above)*

380 'a] *this edn;* a *Q1 (see discussion above)*

382 'a] *this edn;* a *Q1 (see discussion above)*

385 'a] *this edn;* a *Q1 (see discussion above)*

'a] *this edn;* a *Q1 (see discussion above)*

388 SP] *this edn;* Flo. *Q1*; [FLEIRE] *Petter*

gentlewomen] *Nibbe, Petter*; Gentlemen *Q1*

399-400 that he did] *Q1*; what he did *Q2-4*

416 fleet] *Q1-4*; sleet *Petter*

438.1-2 SD] *this edn; Ex. Spe. & Ruf. | Enter Piso and Knight. Q1*

475 turns tail] *this edn;* turnes tayle *Q1 (c), Nibbe*; turnes her tayle *Q1 (u)*

479 'a] *this edn;* a *Q1 (see discussion above)*

480 'a] *this edn;* a *Q1 (see discussion above)*

'em] *this edn;* am *Q1 (see discussion above)*

481 'a] *this edn;* a *Q1 (see discussion above)*

'em] *this edn;* am *Q1 (see discussion above)*

482 'em] *this edn;* am *Q1 (see discussion above)*

483 'em] *this edn;* am *Q1 (see discussion above)*

484 'a] *this edn;* a *Q1 (see discussion above)*

517 SD] *this edn; om. Q1*

520 there] *Q1 (c), Nibbe*; here *Q1 (u)*

520.1-2 SD] *this edn; Exeunt: manet Fleir. Q1*

522 'em] *this edn;* am *Q1 (see discussion above)*

529 oft] *Q2-4*; of *Q1*

532.1 SD] *this edn; Enter the two wenches in boyes apparell. Q1*

552 'em] *this edn;* 'am *Q1 (see discussion above)*

553.1-3 SD] *this edn; Enter Flor, Sparke, Felee: Ruffell, Piso, Knight and Fromaga. Q1*

554 SD] *this edn; om. Q1*

558 which] *Q2-4*; with *Q1*

567 SD] *Petter, Nibbe; om. Q1*

572 SD] *this edn; om. Q1*

574-7 I would … in] *prose Q1; verse Petter*

578 SD] *Petter, Nibbe; om. Q1*

585 SD] *Petter, Nibbe; om. Q1*

590 SD] *this edn; om. Q1*

594 SD] *this edn; om. Q1*

597 SD] *this edn; om. Q1*

599 SD] *this edn; om. Q1*

603 SD] *this edn; om. Q1*

606 SD] *this edn; om. Q1*

607 SD] *this edn; om. Q1*

608 SD] *this edn; om. Q1*

614.1-3 SD] *this edn; Exeunt: manent Piso and Nan. Q1; Q1 places direction at l. 612*

615 SD] *this edn; om. Q1*

618 SD] *Petter; om. Q1*

623.1 SD] *Petter; om. Q1*

624 SD] *Petter; om. Q1*

628 'A dies] *this edn;* Adyes *Q1*; A dyes *Q2-4*

629 'A] *this edn;* A *Q1 (see discussion above)*

631 Contemn] *Q1 (c)*; condemn *Q1 (u)*

632-5 But … harmony] *prose Q1; verse Petter*

3.1

0 [Act 3, Scene 1]] *this edn; Finis Act: Secundi. / Actus Tertius scena prima Q1*

0.1 SD] *this edn; Enter the Ladies each with a Letter, and Fleire aside Q1*

9 'a] *this edn;* a *Q1 (see discussion above)*

10 though] *Q1 (c);* thought *Q1 (u)*

12 SD] *this edn; Change Letters. Q1*

13 SD] *this edn; Reade. Q1*

22 SD] *this edn; Reade. Q1*

29 my] *Q1 (c);* m *Q1 (u)*

30-1 if die, it dies] if dye, it dyes *Q2-3*; if die, it dyes *Q4*; if dye if it dyes *Q1 (c)*; it dye if it dyes *Q1 (u)*

33 zealous] *Q1 (c)*; affectionate *Q1 (u)*

37 'a] *this edn;* a *Q1 (see discussion above)*

42 SP] *this edn*; Fle. *Q1*

44 Then shall] *Q1*; Then it shall *Petter*

54 stands] *Q1*; stand *Petter*

57 'em] *this edn;* a'm *Q1 (see discussion above)*
61 e'en] *this edn;* euen *Q1*
62 Plots] *this edn;* „Plots *Q1*
62.1 SD] *this edn; Exeunt Q1*
73-4 Aye. Who? Aye, aye, aye: 'tis I] *this edn;* I, who? I, I, I,'tis I *Q1*
77 good man] *this edn;* goodman *Q1*
84 Aye] *this edn;* I *Q1*
93 Aye, aye] *this edn;* I, I *Q1*
96 Aye] *this edn;* I *Q1*
102 Aye] *this edn;* I *Q1*
110.1-2 SD] *this edn; Exit Piso: Enter Knight Q1*
128 'a] *this edn;* a *Q1 (see discussion above)*
134 Aye] *this edn;* I *Q1*
166 Aye] *this edn;* I *Q1*
172 SD] *Petter; om. Q1*
179 Aye] *this edn;* I *Q1*
191 Aye] *this edn;* I *Q1*
199 'em] *this edn;* am *Q1 (see discussion above)*
204 Faith, aye.] *this edn;* Faith I. *Q1*

3.2

11 SD] *this edn; om. Q1*
21 peacock] Peacocke *Q2-4*; Peac *Q1 (u)*; Peack *Q1 (c)*
65 SD] *this edn; om. Q1*
69 'em] *this edn;* am *Q1 (see discussion above)*

3.3

0.1-2 SD] *this edn; Enter Fleire one way, Sparke, Ruffell and Petoune another way. Q1*
7 'A] *this edn;* a *Q1 (see discussion above)*
10 'a] *this edn;* a *Q1 (see discussion above)*
11 SD] *this edn; om. Q1*

18 'a] *this edn;* a *Q1 (see discussion above)*
19 'a] *this edn;* a *Q1 (see discussion above)*
'a] *this edn;* a *Q1 (see discussion above)*
21 'a] *this edn;* a *Q1 (see discussion above)*
45 SP] *this edn*; Flo. *Q1*; FLEIRE *Petter*
86 Mushroom] *Mustroome Q1*
87 Señor Fumada] Signior *Fumada Q1*
88 Usquebaugh] Oscabath *Q1*
98 'em] *this edn;* am *Q1 (see discussion above)*
101 SD] *this edn; om. Q1*

4.1

0 [Act 4, Scene 1]] *this edn; Finis Act. Tertii. / Actus Quartus Q1*
0.1-4 SD] *this edn*; *Enter the two Ladies Piso and Knight, and Fromaga one way: Sparke, Ruffell, Petoune and Fleire another way.Q1*
6 SP] *this edn*; Ambo. *Q1*
7 SD] *this edn; om. Q1*
12 SD] *this edn; om. Q1*
26 'a] *this edn;* a *Q1 (see discussion above)*
28 SD] *this edn; om. Q1*
32 SD] *this edn; om. Q1*
54 pray 'e] *this edn;* pra'y *Q1 (see discussion above)*
62 SD] *this edn; om. Q1*
67.1-5 SD] *this edn*; *Exeunt. Manent two Ladies the Lord and Knight: Felicia, and the two Wenches disguised, hide themselues. Q1*
68 SD] *this edn; om. Q1*
74 SD] *this edn; om. Q1*
75 to work] to worke *Q2-4*; so worke *Q1*
79 SD] *this edn; om. Q1*
81 it] *Q2-4*; its *Q1*
82 SD] *this edn; om. Q1*

110 consent] *Q1 (c)*; consenr *Q1 (u)*

115-16 True … secure] *verse Q1, Petter*

142 mingle] *Q3*; mingle mingle *Q1 (u)*; mingle e *Q1 (c)*; mingle, mingle *Q2, 4*; mingle mangle *Petter*

148 Alunio] *Petter*; Aluino *Q1*

150 SD] *this edn; om. Q1*

'a] *this edn;* a *Q1 (see discussion above)*

'a] *this edn;* a *Q1 (see discussion above)*

153.1-2 SD] *this edn; Exeunt. Q1; Petter adds after Exeunt:* [*Enter* FLEIRE *and the two wenches disguised from behind hangings*]

156 virtuous] *Q2-4*; virtuons *Q1*

193 such] *Q2-4*; sueh *Q1*

206 SD] *this edn; om. Q1*

208 SP] *this edn (Leggatt); om. Q1*

4.2

1 eryngo] *this edn;* arringus *Q*

7 my wife were] *Q1(c)*; my were *Q1(u)*; I would mine *Q2-4*

12 pups] *this edn; (Petter);* poops *Q1*

14 spirit] *Q1(c)*; sptrit *Q1(u)*

16 quintessence] Quintessence *Q1(c)*; Quinressence *Q1(u)*

20.1-2 SD] *this edn; Enter Fleire disguised. Q1*

37 Giacomo] *this edn;* Iacomo *Q1*

38 Giacomo] *this edn;* Iacomo *Q1*

43.1 SD] *this edn; Enter Piso and Knight. Q1*

44 SD] *Petter; om. Q1*

47-8 SD] *this edn; om. Q1*; [*To them*] *Petter*

58 taste] *Petter*; tastes *Q1*; tast *Q2-4*

76 'em] *this edn;* a'm *Q1 (see discussion above)*

80 'a] *this edn;* a *Q1 (see discussion above)*

96 SD] *this edn; Exit Q1; Q1 places after l. 95*

98 'em] *this edn;* am *Q1 (see discussion above)*

4.3

7 'a] *this edn;* a *Q1 (see discussion above)*

5.1

0 [Act 5, Scene 1]] *this edn; Actus Quintus Q1*

5.2

0.1-2 SD] *this edn; Enter Fleire at one doore: and a Seruingman at another. Q1*

2 'a] *this edn;* a *Q1 (see discussion above)*

24.1 SD] *this edn; om. Q1;* [*Exit Mittimus.*] *Petter*

28.1 SD] *this edn; Ente: Seruingman with a Ring Q1*

35.1 SD] *this edn; Exeunt severally Q1*

5.3

3-4 By … time] *prose Q1; verse Petter*

7-8 The … worst] *prose Q1; verse Petter*

11-15 Lie … light] *prose Q1; verse Petter*

15 SD] *this edn; om. Q1*

21-3 The … flourish] *prose Q1; verse Petter*

32 Unmask'd] Vnmask't *Q2-3*; Vnmaskt *Q4*; Vnmaske *Q1*

34 None] *this edn;* „None *Q1*

5.4

0.1 SD] *this edn; Enter Fleir, Sparke, and Ruffell. Q1*

15 so] *Q3*; no *Q1-2*; too *Q4*

19 out-drink] *Petter;* drink *Q1*

24 'em] *this edn;* am *Q1 (see discussion above)*

26 apes, man] *Q2-3*; Apes man *Q1, 4*

44 an Inns] an Innes *Q2, 3*; a Innes *Q1, 4*

59 'a] *this edn;* a *Q1 (see discussion above)*

'a] *this edn;* a *Q1 (see discussion above)*

60 'em] *this edn;* am *Q1 (see discussion above)*

61 'em] *this edn;* am *Q1 (see discussion above)*
79 'em] *this edn;* am *Q1 (see discussion above)*
we] *this edn;* wee *Petter*; shee *Q1*
80 'em] *this edn;* am *Q1 (see discussion above)*
83 'em] *this edn;* am *Q1 (see discussion above)*
'em] *this edn;* am *Q1 (see discussion above)*

5.5

0.1-2 SD] *this edn; Enter two Iudges with their traine, and sit down Q1; [A court room.] Enter two* IUDGES [*, one of them* CAIUS,] *with their traine, and sit down Petter*
1 SP] *this edn; Iaylor Q1*
6 SP] *this edn; 2. Iudge Q2-4;* 2. Iudges. *Q1*
8.1 SD] *this edn; Enter a Iaylor. Q1*
9 SP] *this edn; Jaylor Q1*
11.1 SD] *this edn; Enter Fleire like a Doctor. Q1*
20 pray 'e] *this edn;* pra'y *Q1 (see discussion above)*
21 SP] *this edn; Iaylor Q1*
SD] *this edn; om. Q1*
22 forth] *Q2-3*; foorth *Q4*; footh *Q1*
23.1-4 SD] *this edn; Enter Piso Knight, two Ladies, two wenches, Nan and Sue, Petoune, Fromaga Q1*
24 SD] *this edn; om. Q1*
33 ever] ever *Q4*; neuer *Q1-3*
34 even] *Q4*; euen *Q2-3*; enen *Q1*
44 SD] *this edn; om. Q1*
47 SD] *this edn; om. Q1*
55 SD] *this edn; om. Q1*
would'st] *this edn;* wouldst *Q2-4;* wonldst *Q1*
62 SD] *this edn; om. Q1*
63-65 Why … bleed] *prose Q1; verse Petter*
77 SD] *this edn; om. Q1*
79 SD] *this edn; om. Q1*
88 SD] *this edn; om. Q1*

88-9 *Q1* inserts SP before *Is this true*

93.1 SD] *this edn; om. Q1*

99 now] *Nibbe, Petter*; know *Q1*

102 SD] *this edn; om. Q1*

107.1 SD] *this edn; om. Q1*

116 'a] *this edn;* a *Q1 (see discussion above)*

124 'a] *this edn;* a *Q1 (see discussion above)*
'a] *this edn;* a *Q1 (see discussion above)*

129.1 SD] *this edn; om. Q1*

130.1 SD] *Petter (after l. 131); om. Q1*

132 SD] *this edn*; *om. Q1*; [*joining* SPARKE *and* NAN; RUFFEL *and* SUSAN] *Petter (after l. 133)*

134 ev'rything] *this edn;* euerie thing *Q*

137 woo] *this edn*; wooe *Q2-3*; woe *Q1, Q4*

138 SD] *this edn*; *om. Q1*

The Fleire.

Act. 1.

Enter Signior Antifront, with a Lord.

Lord. DEere Lord, I know it well becomes not mee to counſell him that beſt can counſell mee: yet if it pleaſe you but to lend your eares, & heare my loue if not my counſell.

Sig. No more, I know thy loue tends to the ſtopping of my longing and my reſolution : thou knowſt that I no longer now am Signior: Florēce hath got an other gouernor, and one ſtep backe in ſtate of Maieſtie, is a greater fall then to a meaner man that looſeth all: Beſides, thou knowſt our Daughters they are fled, the true inheritors of *Florence* right, and mightie *Piſo* now vſurps our regall ſeate : puiſſant in power and mightie in his wrong, hath mounted Faulcon-like into the sky of ſtate, ſeaz'd on our feeblenes, and beate our weakenes downe. And therefore now I am reſolu'd to finde my two loſt Children out, or like as *Phaeton* in pride did ride, ſo I in grief wil pace the world about.

Lor. Vnto your celſitude I wiſh, till their effects your hopes may neuer faile. *Exit.*

Sig. Farwell, ſome ſtrange diſguiſe I needes muſt take both for my ſtelth away, as for my paſſage on the way: and yet my fortunes fall, diſguiſement is to great if pleaſd the heauens, but their willes ſtill are lawes, all is but Iuſtice & our ſinnes the cauſe: *cuor forte rompe cattiua ſorte.* *Exit.*

B *Enter*

Facsimile of *The Fleer*, sig. B1r
Photograph courtesy of the Beinecke Rare Book and Manuscript Library, Yale University